Autumn 2018

Dear Peggy,

May your deep connection with Spirit always grow, bring you comfort and grant you sustenance.

Fondly,

A UNIVERSE MADE FOR TWO

MOSAICA PRESS

A UNIVERSE MADE FOR TWO

THE GENESIS OF CREATION THROUGH
THE LENS OF TORAH AND NATURE

JACK M. DANIEL

Mosaica Press, Inc.

© 2018 by Jack M. Daniel

Designed by Rayzel Broyde

Typeset by Brocha Mirel Strizower

ISBN-10: 1-946351-09-1

ISBN-13: 978-1-946351-09-8

Published and distributed by:

Mosaica Press, Inc.

www.mosaicapress.com

info@mosaicapress.com

TO MARLENE,
MY AWESOME WIFE.

This book is dedicated by
Steve and Linda Storch
in memory of their parents

BOUROUGH AND LEE STORCH

ברוך ישכר וליבא סטארטש, ז"ל

and

BERNARD AND RUTH SCHWARTZ

דוב ורעכיל שווארץ, ז"ל

They lived modestly and shunned honor, but the joy of
giving and love of others radiated from them always.

הנאהבים והנעימים
בחייהם ובמותם לא נפרדו

It is an honor and privilege to provide my personal dedication to this book. Faith in God and obeying His laws have been guiding principles in my life. It was only in later years that my spiritual awareness was strengthened through more study of His teachings, discussions with spiritual advisers, and personal visits to biblical sites. It was my fortune to meet Mr. Daniel in a medical setting. It quickly became apparent that this man was more than a standard acupuncturist. He was a man of great principle and personal dedication to people and his profession, a person devoted to using the elements of his profession to improve the life and health of his patients. He has accomplished this by interactive dialogue, creative educational seminars, and many technical papers. His completion of this major theological work represents completion of a life goal. In it, he presents theories and conclusions developed from forty-five years of experience and countless hours of in-depth thought and discussion with his patients, peers, and rabbinical leaders. It is my honor to have him as a personal friend and to strengthen my life and faith in my study and use of his work.

DANIEL E. DONOVAN

is a retired Navy Submarine Captain and Communication Specialist. He holds a BS degree in Economics and Naval science from the University of South Carolina and an MS degree in International Affairs from the George Washington University. He is a Distinguished Graduate of the US Naval War College and a graduate of the Industrial College of the Armed Forces. After his Navy service, he completed twenty-six years of industry work in the communication and business fields, and he is a self-published author of several children's books. He and his wife reside in Annapolis, Maryland.

Dedicated by

ANONYMOUS

בס"ד

קהילת בני יעקב שערי ציון
Bnai Jacob Shaarei Zion
Congregation

RABBI MOSHE HAUER

Rabbi Dr. Israel Tabak z"l
Rabbi Joshua Shapiro z"l
Rabbi Dr. Joseph Baumgarten z"l
RABBIS EMERITI

27 Adar, 5778

To my dear friend, *Yedid Nafshi*, Jack, עמו"ש,

I am thrilled to congratulate you on the completion of your outstanding work on the opening verses of the Torah, and to introduce you and your book to your readers. Indeed, this book necessarily invites the reader to join a journey down the roads you have traveled. It is a piece of you, and a perfect illustration of who you are.

The Talmud notes that the inspired *Baal Teshuva* draws and includes every element of his previous life into his newfound world of Torah; every one of his earlier experiences and exposures is used to deepen his present engagement; תשובה מאהבה זדונות נעשו לו כזכיות. Having had the privilege to witness your journey to Torah, I find it remarkable to see how you bring this Talmudic observation to life.

The reader will find expressions of this throughout this book, as you bring together the various strands and stages of your lifetime of curiosity, learning and searching. The result is a three-dimensional work, anchoring and amplifying your study of the sciences and your vast knowledge and experience of Chinese medicine in the eternal words of the Torah.

This is an intense, serious work, and not a casual read. There are elements and ideas expressed here that - as a result of my weaker background in the sciences and my utter ignorance of Chinese thought and medicine - I do not fully comprehend. I nevertheless share this letter, having had the privilege of joining in some of the serious Torah study that produced this volume, and of witnessing your production of this labor of love with diligence, fear of Heaven, and passionate faith.

Typical works of Torah scholarship follow a structured and differentiated path through the generations and stages of Torah teaching and commentary. This path corresponds to the life stages of Torah study, starting with the study of scripture at the age of five, Mishna at ten, and Talmud at fifteen. Here again, your work reflects your own life's path, having entered – or dived into - the world of Torah study as an intelligent and educated adult, drawing at once on any and every element of Torah that you could access. The result is a work that moves uniquely, smoothly and un-self-consciously from the Ramban to Elie Munk, and from the Zohar to the footnotes of the Artscroll Talmud.

Jack, I hope and pray that your work finds an appreciative audience, and – far more importantly – that its completion opens the door for you to the next steps in what we pray will be a very long and fruitful life of continued joyous engagement with the study of Torah, delving ever deeper into its depths, and reveling in the Divine wisdom it grants us. May HKBH grant you and Marlene everything that you wish for with all your hearts and souls. I treasure our friendship.

Warmly,

Rabbi Moshe Hauer

RABBI DAVID E. FINK, Esq.

	BLAUSTEIN BUILDING	
PHONE	SUITE 350	EMAIL
(410) 547-0480	1 N. CHARLES STREET	davidefink@yahoo.com
FAX	BALTIMORE, MARYLAND 21201	WORLD WIDE WEB
(410) 547-7206		www.davidefink.com

February 20 ,2018

I recently completed my second reading of "A Universe Made for Two," a brilliant addition to the lexicon of angles, commentaries, Mesorah and Kabbalah which all contribute to our collective understanding of Hashem's Torah. We know Moshe received the Written Torah at Har Sinai. We also know that the Oral Torah was transmitted verbally from generation to generation. Eventually, the dispersion from Eretz Yisroel caused discrepancies in the Oral Torah, necessitating the writing down of the Mishna and later, even the minute arguments of what was meant in each Mishna were recorded in the form of the Gemara. Many other traditions and mystical knowledge were transmitted as the Kabballah and some of these were similarly alluded to in the Zohar and other Seforim so they would not be lost.

Generations of commentaries gleaned insights into the meaning of Hashem's multifaceted Torah. Rashi, the Ramban, the Rambam, Rabbeinu Yona, the Vilna Gaon and many many others. Indeed, other great Torah scholars like the Baal Shem Tov accentuated alternative aspects of the Torah to spur on generations of Chassidim. At the core of it all though is the truth of Torah. Every Torah giant quoted in a Mishna to every custom adapted by a Gerer Chasid is aimed at preserving Hashem's word. Every secret hinted to in the Zohar to each confrontational logical argument in the Gemara seeks the same thing. This is why we say "Moshe Emes V'Soraso Emes." Not dissimilar from a mathematical theorem, there are often multiple approaches to arriving at the same truth. Challenging equations can be solved by either addition or subtraction or multiplication or division. But they always arrive at the same answer. So it is with Torah, only on an infinitely more complex level. Indeed, one of my great joys is when I see the Baal Haturim understand through Gematria the identical argument between Beis Shammai and Hillel. A coincidence? Of course not! The beautiful, magical, multidimensional Torah. The ultimate Emes. Any Chochma, Math, Science, Language, even Music applied meticulously cannot help but arrive at the same conclusions as Rav Meir and Rebbi Akiva because there is only one Truth.

In "A Universe Made For Two," R' Jack Daniel has unpeeled yet another layer of hidden genius contained within Hashem's Torah. As the Rambam found some utility in portions of Aristotle's philosophy, R' Jack has found deep Torah mysteries hidden and recorded among some of the oldest of recorded world cultures. Indeed, while Yin and Yang may not be studied in the halls of many Yeshivos, they are strikingly similar to the insights of the Ramban into Creation. The average Yeshiva bachur is more familiar with the terminology of Tohu and Vohu than with Hyule, but the Ramban and other Torah Giants were equally intrigued by both and how they related to Maaseh Bereishis. Plasma, matter and black holes may be more commonly referred to in collegiate halls of science but they are also referenced in Kabbalah and the Chinese understanding of the world's creation.

This undertaking adds immeasurably to our appreciation, love and awe of Hashem's Torah. Only the closest of Talmidim to Rashi, his sons-in-law the Baalei Tosfos, were able to gain for us an even greater understanding into Rashi's thoughts, inclusions and omissions. So too, only a student, teacher and master of Chinese philosophy and medicine could uncover for us so many Torah themes and principles hidden within the annals of the ancient Chinese culture and writings.

R' Jack is a brilliant, highly educated, deeply observant and committed Jew. He has worn many hats in my own life. In many ways I have seen him as multifaceted. He has at various times been my Chavrusa, my student, my teacher, my doctor and my close friend. But at the end of the day, our learning has deeply enriched my own love for Hashem's Torah and allowed me to add another layer of richness to my quest to understand more of Hashem's world. I am sure that anyone who reads this masterpiece will find themselves similarly enthralled.

David E. Fink

Congregation
OHR SIMCHA

3209 Fallstaff Road ◆ Baltimore, MD 21215-1720 ◆ www.ohrsimcha.com

בס"ד

Rabbi Ari Storch

Mr. Izzy Alan Hyatt
President

Mr. David Wolf
President Emeritus

Mr. Yehuda Marciano
Vice President

Dr. Moshe Gavant
Chairman of the Board

Mr. Steve Goloskov
Associate Board Member

Mr. David Pfeffer
Associate Board Member,
Gabbai

Mr. Marc Goldenberg
Treasurer

Mr. Jeffrey Goldstein
Event Coordinator

ג' מנחם אב תשע"ה

I recently reviewed Mr. Jack Daniel's phenomenal work, "A Universe Made for Two." I have known Mr. Daniel for many years now; yet, he never ceases to amaze me. Mr. Daniel masterfully synthesizes complicated concepts from astrophysics, Torah, and far eastern wisdom to uncover a uniquely beautiful elucidation of the first days of Creation. Mr. Daniel is skilled at taking these complex ideas and explaining them in ways that even novices can comprehend. I have never seen a comparable work; this *sefer* truly fills a void and enhances Torah understanding. May Mr. Jack Daniel continue to contribute to the world of Torah understanding with future teachings and may he see much success in this and all of his endeavors.

Humbly,

Ari Storch

TABLE OF CONTENTS

SECTION III: APPENDICES

Conceit: an idea; thought; concept. This term is meant to invite the reader into a more sophisticated understanding of the subject of attention.

Elokim (spelled with a *k* in the fourth position): a word substituted for the same word with an *h* appearing in that place. With an *h*, this word is one of God's holy names and as such is not written this way unless in a prayer or scriptural text. It appears numerous times in the following pages.

PREFACE

I'VE BEEN BLESSED with an ability to see common threads of connection extending across widely diverse ideas and branches of knowledge in my attempts to understand the nature of the world around me. I have always desired to know more deeply how things work. My forty-five-year history as a student of Chinese medicine has given me the basis for much of those abilities. Past experiences working as a scientist, along with work in other academic and spiritual endeavors, has sometimes opened my eyes to unusual connections. This unique lens through which I look in attempting to understand things has given me the basic tools for generating this synergistic work. God has given me the life path along which I've come, the accumulation of knowledge I carry with me, and the power to synthesize large and diverse ideas into seamless wholes. I feel compelled to respond to this gift by giving voice to what I've accumulated and integrated about Creation and our world.

I believe certain ideas are worth using to build a cosmology, around which clarity about the manifestations of Nature is brought out. The first and foremost is that since God created a world, His imprint must be found within it. In the vernacular, His fingerprints must be all over it. As this discourse unfolds, I believe you'll see that the archetypes of Creation are evident in the very fabric of the universe. As God is the one Unique One, He used one pattern for the sake of the Genesis of Creation. Therefore, the flowering of all of the diversity of the entire universe must have the signs of God's first creating in them. So, there is one single pattern in the universe and it is able to be found everywhere. In different "locations" it will manifest differently. For example, in a spiral galaxy, the logarithmic spiral is evident in its shape. A logarithmic spiral is also evident in the seed pattern of a sunflower, the sections of a pineapple, or the shape of the mollusk, the chambered nautilus. In each of these instances, the geometry and mathematics of the shapes are identical. Yet, the final product is radically different from instance to instance. It is my firm contention that the one pattern is everywhere and that it manifests in ways that are consistent with the conditions and "places" within which its diverse manifestations appear.

In the summer of 1969, before beginning my last year of college at the University of Connecticut, while I was accumulating a chemistry and biology double major, I attended a lecture on Chinese medicine, with a concentration on the Chinese views of *yin* (陰) and *yang* (陽), by Michio Kushi, a major proponent of macrobiotics in America. For the Chinese, *yin* and *yang* constitute the two polar opposites so easily in evidence in our world in many different features of all existence. He made the assertion that if one could master an understanding of *yin* and *yang*, one could penetrate the secrets of the universe. That lecture initiated a striking change in the trajectory of my life.

That same year, I had come to the conclusion that I needed a way to live that had meaning and purpose beyond the accumulation of college knowledge and the means for a solid livelihood. Three years later, I continued my pursuit of *yin* and *yang* by undertaking a formal course of study in acupuncture at the College of Chinese Acupuncture (UK) in Kenilworth, England. I am now over forty-five years along in practicing and teaching Chinese medicine.

At no time in my upbringing as a Conservative Jew did I become aware of the vastness of the wisdom of the great Jewish Sages, or their practical guidance for living a meaningful life, or the wisdom in setting out the parameters for conduct with one's fellows. Since the trip I took to Israel with my wife and children in 1995, I have turned my life in the direction of being a Torah-observant Jew.

Over ten years ago, I paid a condolence call, as Rabbi Joseph Schecter of Baltimore had passed away. It is common to study a portion of the code of Jewish law during the following year in memory of the person who has passed, and upon my leaving, his son Chaim asked me if I would commit to do this in memory of his father. I demurred but committed to learn the Torah portion of *Bereishit* at the beginning of the book of Genesis. I had no idea what I was getting myself into. I thought I would enjoy and extend my previous comprehension of the mysteries of the universe which I had begun accumulating in 1969. I sought advice from my rabbi, Moshe Hauer, on how to systematically go about doing that. His recommendation, knowing my proclivities for things mystical, was to begin by primarily concentrating on the commentaries on *Bereishit* from the Ramban (Moshe ben Nachman) and Rabbeinu Bachya Ben Asher. Both, respectively, were born and lived in Spain at the end of the twelfth century and the middle of the thirteenth century of the Common Era, and both were acknowledged authorities of *Kabbalah*. It quickly became evident that I needed to significantly narrow my area of concentration because the full exposition of what I had discovered was complete at the conclusion of the second day of Creation. The first two days of *Bereishit* are the sole concentration of this work.

Surprisingly, exposure to the understanding of the Ramban and Rabbeinu Bachya Ben Asher sparked recognition in me that, with deference to all the great scholars and teachers who had preceded me, I, too had something to say about Creation. From whence comes my assertion? I have successfully spent the past forty-five years delving into the workings of the application of *yin* and *yang* in the economy of human health, illness, and healing on an everyday, practical basis, particularly in my work with my patients. In addition, I've delved deeply into attempting to understand the forces of the world's making and unmaking through my formal educational background in the sciences and mathematics. Lastly, for over forty-five years I've taught many hundreds of students about the unfolding of the universe according to the abstractions of *yin* and *yang*.

Essential to the way in which I've addressed the challenges presented by a turn to a Torah life is the recognition that when something like the study of *Bereishit* beckons with the insistence of a "fittingness" to the unfolding of a spiritual life, one must respond with the answer "Yes" to the invitation. Yet, it is with significant trepidation that I approach the writing of this commentary. To express this, I borrow the words of the Ramban, who said in the introduction to his commentary on the Torah, so much more eloquently than I could ever express nor have the right to claim, "I shall begin to write original insights in interpreting the Torah. With fear, with awe, with trepidation, with trembling, with reverence...," and "[M]y wisdom is small and my knowledge is short...," and, finally, "But what shall I do: For my soul yearns for the Torah!"

He concludes his introduction with the following from *Bereishit Rabbah* 8:2:

> *That which is greater than you do not investigate, that which is stronger than you do not probe, that which is beyond you do not seek to know, about that which is concealed from you do not inquire. Contemplate that which you are permitted; you have no concern with hidden matters.*

The exposition and understanding of the first two days of Creation, and how to relate that to how we live our lives, are the essential focus of this work. One might ask how something that is as abstract as a mystical exposition of Creation could lead to anything practical. The applicability produced from an understanding of the first two days of Creation is essential, I believe, to living a peaceful life. Those conclusions, in summary form, are found in appendix B. The complete elucidation of what I've come to understand from the first two days, translated into something that can open doors to the kingdom of self-realization on an everyday level—like a powerful tool come to solve a universal problem, are found in my book, *Abracadbra*, yet to be published.

While being engaged in this research, I have experienced being inexorably drawn to synthesize my career's work and my background in science with the magnificence of the Torah's revelation of the advent of Creation. So onward I have gone, at first just more casually and only for my own gratification, until it became clear that I had no real choice but to commit what I was coming to understand to writing, recording it for others, and, finally, much more recently, realizing that what I had done so far had enough substance to be a book. I've asked myself many times how I could dare undertake to travel seriously into a realm in which the many greats have tread. Those from whom we have writings are the true ancient sages and scholars, including those from cultures other than the Jewish Sages. Put another way, what gives me the right to represent my understanding with enough import to write a book?

I feel compelled and almost as if I've had little choice to write this work. In the context of having been a clinician for over forty-five years, I've come to recognize certain things about myself. The mind that the Sovereign of the universe gave me sees so many connections in the different aspects of human health and illness that it has made me an excellent diagnostician in Chinese medicine. In terms of the study at hand, I can see threads of connection across diverse ideas, disciplines, and approaches. So how do I defend my presumption of worthiness? I consider that I need to respond to this gift by giving a voice to what I've accumulated, and subsequently, presented in this writing. In light of the admonition from *Bereishit Rabbah*, above, about doing so, in writing this book I place myself in jeopardy. However, and at the risk of being considered utterly presumptuous, I reference the Rambam, Moses Maimonides, to defend me in my attempt to elucidate the mysteries of Creation. He says, in the *Moreh Nevuchim* (*The Guide for the Perplexed*), in the introduction to part 3:

> [T]he explanation of these mysteries was always communicated via voce [by mouth]; it was never committed to writing. Such being the case, how can I venture to call your attention to such portions of it as may be known, intelligible and perfectly clear to me? But if, on the other hand, I were to abstain from writing on this subject, according to my knowledge of it, when I die, as I shall inevitably do, that knowledge would die with me, and I would thus inflict great injury on you and all those who are perplexed [by these theological problems]. I would then be guilty of withholding the truth from those to whom it ought to be communicated, and of jealousy depriving the heir of his inheritance. I should in either case be guilty of gross misconduct.

Daniel Pink, in his book, *A Whole New Mind*, asks of his readers to "understand the connections between diverse, and seemingly separate, disciplines. They must know how to link apparently unconnected elements to create something new. And they must become adept at analogy—at seeing one thing in terms of another." He further points out what he calls "pattern recognition," otherwise known as the distinguishing of relationships between relationships; seeing the big picture of associative connections. That is what I am endeavoring to accomplish in this writing.

A few words are in order about the common practice of the Jewish Sages in conveying many important esoteric ideas by alluding to them through what they knew of the sciences of their day. Looking backward with the stunning sophistication of our current models in the sciences, their ideas often seem arcane or downright specious. The same may be true about what I've written here as well sometime in the future. Nevertheless, the value does not lie in whether or not there's a perfect fit or that the science is, in the final analysis, unassailable, but rather, that the allusions yield an elucidation and understanding in a more detailed or perhaps profound way than that which could be expressed without the references to science.

The profundity of the ideational numerical abstractions of One and Two and their interplay is the subject of this book. Maimonides said in *The Guide for the Perplexed*, part 3, chapter 51, and in *Mishneh Torah* 4:10, that those who understand the blending of the natural and the Divine are like royal subjects within the throne room of their exalted king, while those seeking an understanding of the Bible but lacking an understanding of the natural sciences are like subjects groping in vain for the outermost gate of the king's palace. This exploration calls upon the disciplines of Torah exegesis (critical interpretation), Chinese medicine theory, geometry, biology, chemistry, quantum mechanics and particle physics, string theory, astrophysics and cosmology, and *Kabbalah*. The parallels between, intersections of, and illuminations cast from one discipline to another, are the stimulus for the synthesis found within what I've written. May it have merit, help you gain a glimpse into the throne room of the King, and prove worthy of the expenditure of your time.

Baltimore, MD
May 2018

ACKNOWLEDGMENTS

WITH HUMBLE GRATITUDE to God, Who gave me a path to understand deep and profound things, I wish to thank and acknowledge those who have played prominent roles in the process of my having written this work. As well, there are many others, without identifying them, to whom I give my thanks. First, to my parents, Irving and Annette, who gave me consistent support of my decisions of how and where to determine my own future, endorsing and backing my decision to go to England to study acupuncture in 1972, I lovingly give honor and gratitude.

To my wife and life partner, Marlene, for her unswerving support of my growth as a person and as a Jew, as well as the expansion in my devotion to a Torah life, I can only scratch the surface of my deepest appreciation and love.

To our son, Justin, who so prodded me to "true up" the correlations of Torah and science, thank you for your contribution.

To the teachers and mentors of my youth: Mrs. Martin, my childhood librarian, who so beautifully encouraged my love of reading and contributed so mightily to the expansion of my vocabulary. To all of my math and science teachers who engendered a deep appreciation of the order of the universe and the means by which to understand that order. To Michio Kushi, who, that fateful summer evening, sparked the beginning of my pursuit of the secrets of *yin* and *yang*. To J.R. Worsley, my first acupuncture teacher, who taught me to see the display of wholeness in a person's health, and from whom I began to deeply recognize the mystery of human life. To Manfred Porkert, who bequeathed a special understanding of Chinese medicine to me, I give my thanks. To Fr. Claude Larre and Elisabeth Rochat de la Vallée, from whom I learned the true depth of Chinese medicine and from whom I understood the power of numbers.

To Rabbi Binyomin Field, my first learning partner in Torah, for patiently guiding a novice along an ancient and profound path, I give my deep appreciation.

To Rabbi Moshe Hauer, for his loving encouragement for my pursuing *Bereishit* in what merely began as a "project," and who permitted me to use him as a sounding board for my perspectives. His devotion to me finishing the manuscript was above and beyond.

To Chaim Schecter, son of Rabbi Joseph Schecter, who, during his father's *shivah*, agreed to accept my offer to learn *Bereishit* for the following year to honor his father's memory. In addition, I give my gratitude to Chaim for asking that fateful question, "So what?" when I excitedly shared some of my ideas along the way. His question opened the possibility for my book, *Abracadbra*, and the development of my workshop entitled "Trust, Forgiveness and the Path to Peace™." The essentials of *Abracadabra* and the workshop can be found in appendix B.

To my dear friend, Dovid Fink, a wonderful Torah scholar, who has enthusiastically received my ideas and has been so highly encouraging of my carrying on the work of this writing, I give my thanks for our conversations and friendship.

To Paul Volosov, with whom, in our study of the Maharal in *Gur Aryeh*, I found such tremendous validation for the most important of the premises in this book. Our stimulating conversations have been truly inspiring.

To those friends and acquaintances who so enthusiastically heard the skeleton description of what I've been writing, I give my gratitude for the fuel with which they all provided me. Of course, these acknowledgments wouldn't be valid without me expressing my appreciation, respect, and admiration for all of the ancient sages who have delved into the mysteries of Creation and left their legacies of understanding for all of us. It is in their footsteps I follow, far behind.

THE DEFINITION OF "YIN" AND "YANG"

FOR THE SAKE of making clarity in the face of possible misunderstanding, this introduction should provide the proper orientation to the development of the text. I describe the duality of the physical world using the terms *yin* and *yang*—useful conceptual tools I first encountered during my training in Chinese medicine. *Yin* and *yang* are technical Chinese terms used to describe inherent opposites that are at the same time complementary. The terms *yin* and *yang* are used in my writing solely as properties of any dynamic system of a dual-character nature.

The symbol of yin and yang

This symbol is used to depict the opposing yet complementary dynamic forces of a dual system. The symbol itself is striking in how much information it conveys about the complex interrelationship between seemingly opposite forces. While it is true that this form has been appropriated for use by Eastern religious disciplines, its use to describe natural phenomena long predates its appropriation by any theological cause. I never use these terms or their associated symbol to recognize or associate with any Eastern religious practices or beliefs or *avodah zarah*, Heaven forbid.

There simply are no equivalent English or Hebrew words or phrases which so efficiently capture the nature of this relationship—opposite, yet also mutually interdependent—as efficiently as the Chinese *yin* and *yang*. However, it is important, given the ways in which the etymological meaning was appropriated by Eastern religions, to draw a very clear distinction between my usage of *yin* and *yang* as descriptors of natural phenomena and their usage in a religious context. The references to these two terms in my writing, *A Universe Made for Two*, are intended exclusively to describe natural phenomena and their underlying abstractions. The meaning of these terms is found within the Chinese characters. The Chinese character for *yang* is 陽, representing the properties associated with the sunny side of the hill. The Chinese character for *yin* is 陰, representing the dynamism inherent in the phenomena associated with the shady side of the hill.

The nature of the sunny side of the hill is as follows: The air and soil will be warmer. Warmer air will expand and flow upward and the entire landscape will be brighter. The opposite will take place on the shady side: the air will be colder, denser, darker, and inclined to sink. On the sunny side, the air will tend to be drier than its counterpart; the shady side will feel damper. These two contrasting sets of qualities are fundamentally intertwined due to the topography of the landscape. They cannot be separated from one another because they do not exist independently of one another. In my writing, I use *yin* and *yang* not in any religious context whatsoever, but exclusively as the most precise way to describe the dual-natured opposites that comprise the universe, as adjectives describing complementary opposites in a well-coordinated dynamic system.

There is precedent in works of Jewish religious scholarship for the usage of secular terminology from other languages to help describe various phenomena. For example, in describing the process of Creation, the Ramban discusses the Greek term *hyule*, about which he speaks at length in his Torah commentary. The Ramban describes the advent of *hyule* this way: "[B]rought into being from complete, absolute nihility an exceedingly fine primary essence with no substance." Following, the Ramban says, "This is the primary substance called by the Greeks *hyule*. And after this *hyule*, [God] did not create (*bara*) anything." He also says, "You should know that heaven and all that is within are one substance, and earth and all that is within are one substance. The Holy One, blessed is He, created both of these from nothing. These two things alone were created, and everything else is made from them. Now this substance is that which the Greeks called *hyule*." Therefore, two *hyule* are created, *ex nihilo*. Finally, about this the Ramban goes on to state, "God created (out of nothing) heaven, for He brought heaven's (primary) matter (*hyule*) into existence out of nothing, and earth, for He brought earth's (primary) matter (*hyule*) into existence out of nothing (as well)."

The expression of the elements of nature as having a dichotomous relationship is not new to Jewish scholarship either. Rabbi Elie Munk, commenting on *Parashat Mishpatim* 22:17, says in his Torah commentary, "The elements of nature revolve around a negative pole and a positive pole, and this division spans the whole of creation." This is the exact orientation in what I have written. *Yin* and *yang* are simply the most concise terms to describe this state.

BEFORE COMMENCING

CHAPTER ONE

OVERVIEW

ONE COULD ASK, "What is the reason for the focus on only the first two days in the Creation story?" First of all, it is well beyond a story. The very letters and words of the Torah are serving as the path for us to have insight into the nature of human existence and the nature of our partnership with God in the perpetual creating of the world. That my concentration is only on the first two days in this exposition is a statement about the meaning of the ideational abstraction which is recognizable as the number two. The abstraction of "two-ness" was, for the sake of the creation of our world (without commenting on a question about alternate or parallel universes), a "necessity." Tautologically, this is obvious in the face of the pervasive, observable pairings of virtually all phenomena in our time- and space-bound world: up/down, inside/outside, night/day, matter/anti-matter, female/male, and so on, virtually ad infinitum. Only with the advent of the creation of the ideational abstraction of two-ness did God create anything distinct from His One-ness, and only then could duality come into existence and persist. Within unity, nothing separate or distinct can come into existence or persist, whatever it may be, when its independent existence is instantly swallowed up by God's omnipresent unity, causing it to cease to exist as a distinct "something."

The word *tzimtzum* means self-limitation or withdrawal (also, restriction or contraction). *Kabbalah* attributes the term *tzimtzum* to what God did in order to create the vacated space, called *challal*, into which God then created the world. This was at the very kernel of the beginning in the Creation process of bringing the world into existence. The essence of this "act" of *tzimtzum* was essentially that of God creating "not-Himself," by withdrawing or restricting His light "to the sides of a conceptual space." The *tzimtzum* is bounded, and, therefore, limited; it is the exact opposite state of God's infinite, all-pervasive omnipresence. This operational negation of His own Oneness was the necessary condition in order for our world to be created and for it to be able to persist in time and space.

In *gematria* (wherein all Hebrew letters have a numerical value), the Hebrew letter *bet* has the value of two, the number of duality. This duality is then revealed in the pattern embedded throughout Creation. Rabbi Elie Munk, commenting on *Parashat Mishpatim* 22:17, says in his Torah commentary, "The elements of nature revolve around a negative pole and a positive pole, and this division spans the whole of creation." This condition of duality is established in the first two days of the account of Creation found in Genesis. I find it both starkly obvious, and yet surprising, that the first two days are about the unfolding of the ideational abstraction of two. It's almost as if the truth about our temporal world has been hiding in plain sight, winking at us, since the giving of the Torah at Mount Sinai. Days One and Two are sufficient to give us the keys to the kingdom of self-actualization; living as we do in lives of spirit and matter. The announcement being made is that all to follow is a description of the procession from unity to duality and its manifestations.

For a novel discussion of the letter construction of the word *tzimtzum*, please refer to appendix C.

CHAPTER TWO

THE INCEPTION OF DUALITY

THE FIRST LETTER of the Torah, the *bet* (ב), has the *gematria* of two. Throughout the ages, many commentators have asked about the significance of its extra-large size on the parchment of a Torah scroll, and the answers vary. Taken in the context of the full verse at the very beginning of Genesis, however, I will assert that this large *bet* signifies the "announcement" of the inception of the ideational abstraction of duality (and, hence, according to the Talmud,[1] of any multiplicity). Referencing *Bereshit Rabbah*, author Michael J. Alter writes:

> "[S]tipulates that the primordial Torah was written with black fire on white....Before it was [is] possible to create a multi-discrete world, it was [is] first necessary to establish the possibility of contrast. The imagery of black fire on white, sufficiently dramatizes the concept of contrast, as does the Torah written with black letters on white parchment."[2]

This state of contrast, being the essence of duality, then determines everything else that manifests which flows from the first two days of Creation. The shape of the letter *bet* (ב), almost like an open mouth in the act of speaking, opens toward the text that follows. This is a

---

1   Eliezer Herzka, *The Gemara: Tractate Yoma* (Brooklyn: Mesorah, 1998), vol. II, ch. 5, 62b¹, fn. 2.
2   Michael J. Alter, *Why the Torah Begins with the Letter Beit* (Northvale: Aronson, 1998), p. 58, fn. 32.

declaration that the first two days of Creation are the exposition of the unfolding of the nature of duality itself. This takes place through the power of the generative capacity of the normative, definitional, ideational abstraction "two," the progenitor of duality.

In Aryeh Kaplan's introduction to his translation of the *Bahir*, whose authorship is attributed to *Neḥunya Ben Ha-Kanah*, he refers to Isaac Luria's *Etz Chaim*, in which it is said that God's first act in Creation was to create the *tzimtzum*, the vacated space. The essence of this first creation was the act of God "constricting His light to the sides" from some "portion" of Himself, to produce a space devoid of His light (thereby, in effect, creating "not-Himself"). This is sometimes referred to as God having created a "conceptual space" into which He could create Creation. It resulted in what is known as the *challal* (חלל), the spiritual void, described as a Divinely-specified ball-like hollow of perfect sphericity. In the cosmological terms of modern physics, this description is completely congruent with the nature of a black hole. In later chapters, we'll establish further support for the notion that the *bet* itself founds the advent of the original singularity from which all of Creation exploded in the Big Bang.

The *shoresh* or word-root of *challal* is ח-ל-ל, and also means desecration. At the very first, God created a unique "one," the *tzimtzum,* that was not-Himself, devoid of Himself (actually His light) and, therefore, that was the essence of desecration. It held the promise of a non-eternal Creation, devoid of the Infinite light of the *Ein Sof,* and the possibility of a non-good, temporal world. Within this void, and only within this absence of God's pure, undiluted light, could the condition of free will exist. We say in the morning's prayer liturgy from Isaiah (45:7), "He forms light and creates darkness." This *choshech* (darkness) of Creation has to be a "palpable" darkness, a creation of near-infinite density (a singularity of near-infinite density in astrophysics is a black hole), a perfectly dark creation, since it is the opposite of the ineffable nature of God's light. It is also said in Isaiah (ibid.) that God "makes peace and creates evil," which is for most of us a deeply troubling notion. But in the sense that I am describing here, evil isn't bad! It is solely the absence of God's infinite light. Further, by virtue of that, it is *the* necessary condition for the advent of free will. Therefore, if you'll pardon the expression, it is the essential, necessary evil in the creation of the world. As noted a moment ago and to be supported in later chapters, this is **the** singularity. This is the original singularity, the first and only single primordial black hole, out of which the entire universe sprang in one burst of manifestation.

In this context, we can now understand that the *challal* was pure evil, a true *chillul Hashem* (desecration of God). Only God could eradicate and desecrate His own light (obviously, not actually possible, since God can't kill Himself, etc.). So, God (One) created one, the singularly unique creation of the *challal*, vacant of His light, a single unique Creation, the *tzimtzum*; the "mother" of all black holes. This is the perfect darkness, the epitome of evil, since God (His light) is not "there."

This notion requires a different look at the nature of evil. This, just perhaps, illuminates why the *nachash* (the serpent in the Garden of Eden) *had* to be in the Garden and why it was destined to seduce Eve into performing an act in direct contradiction to God's command. Adam and Chavah (Adam and Eve) *had* to eat from the Tree of the Knowledge of good and evil in order to be fully enabled with the power of choice. After, as the snake says to Chavah, if they were then to eat from the *Eitz HaChayim* as well, they would know good and evil *and* be immortal. However, this would be an impossibility, given the boundaries of time and space of the world and everything in it. By knowing good and evil, further enabling themselves to be truly made in the image of God, *b'tzelem Elokim* (more later on the Distinguisher of Distinctions), Adam and Chavah stepped into the possibility of being like God, made in His image, with the power to designate distinctions and generate the advent of opposites, thereby securing for themselves their free will, just without the immortality.

When One created one, the two could bring all multiplicity into existence. The birth of the archetype of duality was born. In the absence of God's withdrawing Himself from Himself, His unity would overwhelm and obliterate any boundedness, and all would revert to oneness again. In order for the vacated space to occur and persist, (being perpetually created, newly, in every microsecond of existence), a condition would have had to come into being which preceded the advent of the *tzimtzum* and that, I'll assert here, was God's generation of the ideational abstraction of duality: "two-ness."

Regressively, we'll consider that what "precedes" the generation of duality is actually the act of creating distinctions. Out of the *Ein Sof*, the monolithic infinitude of God, only creating the ideational abstraction of distinctions could lead to the advent of duality. In the field of God's oneness, only in distinguishing out the distinction of distinctions as an ideational abstraction could the persistence of self and not-self come into existence. At the outset, the creation of something out of "everything—no-thing," the drawing out of something from the field of all possibilities (creation *ex nihilo, yeish me'ayin*, something from nothing) rests on the capacity to distinguish distinctions. The totality of everything, when as yet undistinguished, is no-thing. Within the Infinite One, all-and-everything exists simultaneously in no-time and no-space. It is all undistinguished (undifferentiated). God's act of distinguishing out something from "everything—no-thing" causes its existence to spring into being. As the Ramban quotes from the *Sefer Yetzirah*, "[A]nd thus made that which was a nothing, something." Akin to this is the famous visual paradox wherein the question, "Is it a vase or two faces?" presents itself. Only when we notice the two faces do they "exist" for us. Before that, the vase calls for our attention more readily. Which is it? Or is it both? The point is that once something becomes distinct, it exists. Until then, it is simply is part of the background. This is stunningly revealed in the following anecdote from Jill Bolte Taylor's brilliant book, *My Stroke of Insight*. In it, she recounts her experience of her left hemisphere stroke and the shutting-down process of her distinction-making left hemisphere's function. In later chapters, she describes the rehabilitation of this distinguishing out of distinctions that that hemisphere produces. She

describes as follows, on p. 99, while relearning to put together a child's jigsaw puzzle:

> *Mama watched me very closely and realized that I was trying to fit pieces together that obviously did not belong together based upon the image on their front side. In an effort to help me, (she) noted, "Jill, you can use color as a clue." I thought to myself, Color, color, and like a light bulb going off in my head, I could suddenly see color...It still blows my mind (so to speak) that I could not see color until I was told that color was a tool I could use. Who would have guessed that my left hemisphere needed to be told about color in order for it to register.*

Literally, until the linguistic distinction "color" came back into existence triggered by her mother's prompting, the experience of distinguishing colors *did not exist for her*!

For the ancient Chinese, *yin* (陰) and *yang* (陽) were the two generative primal forces of duality in the created world. The Chinese character for *yin* represents the shady side of the hill and is the contractive, centralizing, condensing force (among other labels of description) of the universe. The Chinese character for *yang* is the sunny side of the hill and is the expansive, distributing, dispersing force of the universe. They are complementary and opposite, mutually interdependent and inter-transformational. This makes them the rock bottom, fundamental qualities (non-physical ones) of all multiplicity in the manifest and un-manifest world. They are the Chinese matches to the Greek notion of *hyule* (or *hylē*) (ὕλη), spoken of by the Rambam, Rabbeinu Bachya ben Asher, and the Ramban, as the two substances (actually substance-less substances) that were created (*bara*) out of nothing, at the very first, from which God made everything else. I'll say more about this in the discussion about the First Day, *yom echad*.

Qi (氣), pronounced *chee*, is the term applied to the resultant of the interplay of the forces of *yin* (陰) and *yang* (陽) and is the animating force for all dynamism in the universe. It has particular qualities when it is associated with human life; for us, it is that without which we do not live. The Chinese character for *qi* depicts a cooking pot with rice cooking inside, and shows the lid jiggling away as the rice is cooking. The emphasis in the character is the movement generated by the steam that is jiggling the lid over the cooking rice. Movement is synonymous with *qi*. The closest cognate in Hebrew would be *ruach* (רוח), in Latin it would be *pneuma*.

While the first utterance we see in Genesis is *"Va'yomer Elokim yehi ohr, va'yehi ohr,"* I am asserting that the act of creating distinctions—the advent of distinguishing out the abstract distinction of distinctions—precedes virtually all other acts in the process of Creation. However, we're going to say that "prior" to this was (is) the act of creating "creating" itself—the generative power of God's bringing a unique something into existence out of His unity. To create, the Creator has to have the capacity to create. Therefore, of necessity, creation by God must always be creation *ex nihilo*, or *yeish me'ayin*, consequently producing something from no-thing. (That is, God is transcendent of all constraints of time and space, spanning past, present, and future simultaneously in a condition of no-time/no-space.) "No-thing" directly implies the designation of "everything," as in this world of God's existence, within perfect unity, all and everything is undifferentiated. Everything (therefore, no-thing) exists simultaneously, time and space having no meaning in God's world. This rests on the understanding that the omnipresent Being is total, and that, as the *Rambam* says in his Thirteen Articles of Faith, there can be no other. However, Creation inserts other-ness instantly, as the implication is that Creation generates subject and object as its very essence. Thus, creating "creating" is the prime distinguisher of all distinctions in the universe. Aryeh Kaplan says this in a slightly different way: "First He created the will to create."[3]

This creating of the distinguishing of the distinction of distinctions, as a primal ideational archetype, even though it is not recorded in the Torah, is given prominence and is exemplified by the *bet* at the beginning of Genesis (בראשית). The shape of the letter *bet*, coupled with the

---

3   Aryeh Kaplan, *Innerspace* (Jerusalem: Moznaim, 1990), p. 104.

implied direction of what it encompasses (←ב), which seems to enclose the text to its left (right to left in Hebrew), indicates that everything that follows is a description of the nature of two-ness. This is equivalent to the bringing into existence the abstraction of distinctions. It is an announcement declaring the nature of duality and the coming into existence of a binary world. Our Jewish Sages discuss that the beginning of the Torah might have begun with the first letter, *aleph* (א), having the *gematria* of one. The reason, we'll maintain, that it was not is that the Torah itself was originated by God, before the advent of Creation, and that one, unity, *aleph* (א), exists as the Field of unity from which all distinctions spring. Only One could (can) create two out of unity (everything—no-thing; creation ex *nihilo* [*yeish me'ayin*]). That came as a result of the distinguishing out of "distinctions" as a fundamental, organizational, ideational abstraction of the entire universe; resulting in the unfoldment of all of space-time.[4] In physical terms, the unfolding emanates from the initial singularity of the primal black hole.

The first word of the Torah, *bereishit* (בראשית), is composed of six letters and is mostly (mis)translated as "in the beginning." Actually, the grammar of *bereishit* cannot mean this. Rabbi Moshe M. Eisemann says about the first verse of the Torah, "[W]e now know that there is no *p'shat* (simple meaning) to this *pasuk* (verse)."[5] He goes on to say that "*derash* (interpretation) has the field to itself." So, employing a widely accepted kabbalistic convention of assigning special attention to three-letter words, *bereishit* transforms itself into these two three-letter words: *bara shēt* (ברא שית). The Ramban refers to this approach in the introduction to his Torah commentary. Reference to this convention is also found in the Talmud (e.g., *Sukkah* 49a). The verb *bara* (ברא), "He created," is reserved for God alone and refers only to creation ex *nihilo*; creation of something from nothing (no-thing), *yeish me'ayin*. On adopting the three-letter word convention, the first verse of Genesis becomes: *Bara*

---

4   In current theoretical physics, space and time emerged from the primordial fireball simultaneously, and the term space-time is a designation of the "fabric" of the universe. These constitute the four dimensions of our universe: length, width, depth, and time.

5   Moshe M. Eisemann, *For Rashi's Thoughtful Students* (Baltimore: Eisemann, 2010), pp. 61–63.

shēt bara Elokim et ha'shamayim v'et ha'aretz (ברא [בראשית] שית ברא
אלקים את השמים ואת הארץ). The word אלקים (spelled with a ק [*qof*]) is a
word substituted for the same word with a ה [*hei*] appearing in its place.
This word is one of God's holy names and as such is not written with its
normal ה unless in a prayer or scriptural text. This is the convention we
will use throughout.

At first it would appear that with the advent of two iterations of
the word *bara,* one following the other, there are **two** creations *ex
nihilo*: "*Bara shēt bara Elokim....*" This impossibility—of two creations
ex nihilo—must be reconciled. Obviously, if one creation *ex nihilo* exists, another is, of necessity, precluded from all possibilities. What we
must find here, instead, is actually one creation *ex nihilo*, with multiple
features, aspects, or facets being described simultaneously—**not** a
chronology, **not** a sequence, and **not** a chain of cause and effect.

Shēt (שית), in the statement "*bara shēt,*" has two relevant translations
in this context: "six" and "foundation." I am proposing a conflated
interpretation and translation. Holding both meanings as being valid
simultaneously, I'm asserting that the Torah is declaring, "He created
the foundation of six." That is, the abstractions of foundation and six
are intimately related in the account of Creation and together are required to give us our world as it is configured, physically and mystically.
Additionally, "foundation" refers to the infinitely small speck discussed
by Rabbeinu Bachya ben Asher and the Ramban.

This speck is also discussed in Brian Green's book *The Elegant Universe*,
an exploration of modern physics' understanding of string theory. He
refers to the speck (without his actually naming it as such, but the term
applies nevertheless) when he recounts the description of the original
singularity, the primordial black hole, and its indescribably miniscule
size. In addition, this sets us looking in the direction of the smallest
distance in the history of the universe which is described in string theory: the Planck length (named after the physicist Max Planck). This is
the finite but virtually infinitely small (less than 10^{-33} cm) length of the
vibrating loops of "strings" that make up the fundamental subatomic
particles and forces in the modified standard model of our current

physics cosmology. String theory is the closest physics has yet come to a unifying principle, bringing together and then reconciling the contradictions inherent in the merging of the fields of relativity theory and quantum physics. This speck was brought into existence at the onset of Creation and it is that from which the entire universe then expanded. There are references in Scripture that equate that speck with the stone on the Temple Mount in Jerusalem, called the Shettiah Stone (אבן שתייה or אבן שתיה), upon which the Holy of Holies in the ancient Jerusalem Temple was located. Rabbeinu Bachya ben Asher asserts that this is the "place" (the actual point) from which the entire universe was founded and expanded. The parallels of Torah and modern physics are showing themselves to be strikingly similar.

For the moment, focusing in narrowly, we'll take it that the number six refers to the six directions of three-dimensional space, as the Maharal of Prague discusses. While he does not designate position in relation to the six directions, they are, or will be seen to be, clearly, front/back, left/right, and up/down. The number six has many manifestations in our world, all constituitive of the construction of a world perfectly suited for human life. The *Bahir* describes the *tzimtzum* as a perfect sphere. This is consistent with the position that the Maharal takes about the six directions, as those six directions, when expanded out equidistantly from a single point, will meet a sphere at its circumference. Obviously, since no actual physical space exists at the advent of the *tzimtzum*, what's really being described is the ideational abstraction of perfect sphericity. This is the archetype, if you will, that will generate a perfect sphere in the physical world with its inherent properties, wherein the mathematical symbol for the degree of sphericity, equals one ($\Psi = 1$). When a sphere is projected onto a plane, or if we intersect a sphere with a plane, the resultant is a perfect circle (see appendix A). The geometry of the circle is unique.

Properties like Pi (π), radian measure, the study of trigonometry, wheels, balls, and the spreading circles in a pond produced by a single drop of water hitting the surface, all stem from the inherent properties of the sphere and circle. Put another way, the abstraction of six is constitutive of the nature of the sphere and the circle and inheres in the essence of God's created world. For example, there are an infinite number of circles in a perfect sphere, each one of which, in the context of simple planar geometry, will generate six circles around itself in perfect contiguity. More will be said later as to the implications and meaning of the array of a central seventh circle surrounded by six circles of exactly

the same diameter. All of this infers that the *tzimt-zum* itself either generates the number six or is inherently linked with six or comes from the abstraction of six-ness. Or, all of those descriptions are true simultaneously. Additionally, one sphere surrounds itself perfectly with 12 other spheres of exactly the same diameter, a further iteration of the number six. Further, according to Mario Livio, the number six is the first "perfect number,"[6] perfect numbers being composed of the sum of all the smaller numbers that divide into it (in this instance: 6 = 1 + 2 + 3), while being equal to the sum of the smaller numbers multiplied by each other too. The notion of a perfect number was special to the ancient geometers and mathematicians.

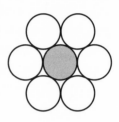

Chinese medicine, within which the terms *yin* and *yang* are crucial to understanding the workings of human health, is the longest continuously practiced system of medicine in the history of humanity. Its effectiveness and successes have spanned continents and millennia. There are striking similarities within Chinese medicine to kabbalistic thought. The Chinese made meticulous compilations over many centuries by observing the workings of nature (*teva*). The detailed and recorded inspection of nature generated the tools of *yin* and *yang* we're using in this writing.

The prominent *bet* at the beginning of the Torah is announcing the instigation of duality, the creation of the distinction of distinctions. As the account of Creation proceeds at the beginning of Genesis, the

---

6   Mario Livio, *The Golden Ratio* (New York: Broadway, 2002), p. 33.

a priori condition entirely necessary to the first word is God's oneness. For the first distinction to arise, that distinction being the act of distinguishing distinctions, it is clear that directly "above" it is the creating of creating, and still superior, unity itself, the limitless Infinite One. There lies the place of the *aleph*, the field of oneness out of which duality processes. **One** stands behind the Torah. It couldn't be at the head of the Torah, as the first verse is about the essence of, and process of, the manifestation of duality.

The declaration found in the first few verses is of the archetypal description and allusion to the dual nature of the universe: from One (Hashem), then one (*tzimtzum*) which then proceeds to two. Slightly as an aside but serving to bolster the evidence for the power inherent in this number, another manifestation of the interpenetrating reality of the nature of two-ness is the nature of magnetic fields. No magnetic field has ever been found or created with other than two poles.

Parenthetically, the progression from One to one is consistent with the first few digits in the Fibonacci series, a famous mathematical progression. This series is the one in which each new number in the series is the sum of the two most proximate preceding numbers: 1, 1, 2, 3, 5, 8, 13, 21, etc. The ratio of any two successive numbers, where the larger is divided by the smaller, approaches more and more nearly to the number known as *Phi* (Φ), whose numerical value is an irrational number like Pi (π has a value of approximately 3.14159) and is equal to approximately 1.618. *Phi* is also known as the Golden Number and, in physical terms, describes the nature of the spirals (referred to earlier in the preface) that are found in galaxies, pineapples, pine cones, sunflowers, etc. We'll speak more of this later, but for the most elaborate treatment of this subject, please refer to *The Golden Ratio*.[7]

Now we return for a moment to the discussion of string theory, also called superstring theory by some. The essence of it is the following: All fundamental subatomic particles and forces (all reduced to being called particles) are made of vibrating, indescribably thin, filamentous loops,

---

7   By Mario Livio.

which have come to be called "strings." A string as described has an inherently vibratory nature. Thus, we have a two-dimensional "structure" that expands itself into a third dimension as it moves in a pattern of vibration. It is the vibrating oscillations in frequency and amplitude which determine the particles that correspond with them. Frequency is *yin* and amplitude is *yang*. *Yin* is the horizontal axis and *yang* is the vertical axis. This is definitional.

Some of those particles have a mass of zero, like the photon, effectively rendering them as forces, and some actually have mass, rendering them as particles, like electrons or a neutrino. Given the nature of the two parameters of frequency and amplitude, we can see that the number two is at work here in this fundamental view of the structure of reality in this universe. This, of course, is nothing other than the workings of duality through the offices of *yin* and *yang*.

To return to the conundrum of the apparency of two creations *ex nihilo*, if we drain the verse of any implied reference to time or its passage or of anything of a sequential nature, we see that both instances of the verb *bara* (ברא) are only one act, with two different features being declared together. Thus, the first verse in Genesis reads, "*Bara shēt bara Elokim et ha'shamayim v'et ha'aretz*" (ברא שית ברא אלקים את השמים ואת הארץ), which then translates as, "He created the foundation of six, He created *Elokim*, the heavens and the earth."

We'll now look at the individual words, phrases, verses, and days in greater detail. This includes analyzing the juxtapositions of letters, phrases, and verses, all held within the context of each day and within the context of the two days taken together and as a whole. Henceforward in this writing, "day" will be referred to as *yom* and "days" will be referred to as *yamim*, for reasons that will be abundantly clear as we go along. A *yom* is most commonly associated with the passage of measured time. For the purpose of this writing, in the abstract, I'm treating a *yom* as a distinct segment in a progression.

THE VERSES, PHRASES, WORDS, AND LETTERS OF THE FIRST TWO DAYS (YAMIM) OF CREATION

בְּרֵאשִׁית (בראשית) בָּרָא אֱלֹקִים אֵת הַשָּׁמַיִם וְאֵת הָאָרֶץ. וְהָאָרֶץ הָיְתָה תֹהוּ וָבֹהוּ וְחֹשֶׁךְ עַל פְּנֵי תְהוֹם וְרוּחַ אֱלֹקִים מְרַחֶפֶת עַל פְּנֵי הַמָּיִם. וַיֹּאמֶר אֱלֹקִים יְהִי אוֹר וַיְהִי אוֹר וַיַּרְא אֱלֹקִים אֶת הָאוֹר כִּי טוֹב וַיַּבְדֵּל אֱלֹקִים בֵּין הָאוֹר וּבֵין הַחֹשֶׁךְ. וַיִּקְרָא אֱלֹקִים לָאוֹר יוֹם וְלַחֹשֶׁךְ קָרָא לַיְלָה וַיְהִי עֶרֶב וַיְהִי בֹקֶר יוֹם אֶחָד.

וַיֹּאמֶר אֱלֹקִים יְהִי רָקִיעַ בְּתוֹךְ הַמָּיִם וִיהִי מַבְדִּיל בֵּין מַיִם לָמָיִם. וַיַּעַשׂ אֱלֹקִים אֶת הָרָקִיעַ וַיַּבְדֵּל בֵּין הַמַּיִם אֲשֶׁר מִתַּחַת לָרָקִיעַ וּבֵין הַמַּיִם אֲשֶׁר מֵעַל לָרָקִיעַ וַיְהִי כֵן. וַיִּקְרָא אֱלֹקִים לָרָקִיעַ שָׁמָיִם וַיְהִי עֶרֶב וַיְהִי בֹקֶר יוֹם שֵׁנִי.

CHAPTER THREE

YOM ECHAD: FIRST VERSE, FIRST CONCEIT

בְּרֵא שִׁית (בְּרֵאשִׁית) בְּרָא אֱלֹקִים אֵת הַשָּׁמַיִם וְאֵת הָאָרֶץ. וְהָאָרֶץ הָיְתָה תֹהוּ וָבֹהוּ וְחֹשֶׁךְ עַל פְּנֵי תְהוֹם וְרוּחַ אֱלֹקִים מְרַחֶפֶת עַל פְּנֵי הַמָּיִם. וַיֹּאמֶר אֱלֹקִים יְהִי אוֹר וַיְהִי אוֹר. וַיַּרְא אֱלֹקִים אֶת הָאוֹר כִּי טוֹב וַיַּבְדֵּל אֱלֹקִים בֵּין הָאוֹר וּבֵין הַחֹשֶׁךְ. וַיִּקְרָא אֱלֹקִים לָאוֹר יוֹם וְלַחֹשֶׁךְ קָרָא לָיְלָה וַיְהִי עֶרֶב וַיְהִי בֹקֶר יוֹם אֶחָד.

FIRST VERSE

בְּרֵא שִׁית (בְּרֵאשִׁית) בְּרָא אֱלֹקִים אֵת הַשָּׁמַיִם וְאֵת הָאָרֶץ.

In my reading of this verse, the following is the most illuminating translation: "He created the foundation of six, He created *Elokim*, and heaven and earth." What this means in simplest terms is that God created from absolute nihility the ideational abstractions necessary for creating a world bounded by the constraints of duality, represented by the fundamental, abstract, ideational distinctions of foundation, six, (His attribute of) *Elokim*, heaven and earth. Many of these terms are normative, operational definitions and descriptions of archetypical, ideational abstractions. Whenever a word is presented in the Torah for the first time, it is considered to be an archetype that determines how it can be taken later as the word is used again. Archetypal, ideational abstractions are like fundamental shaping forces that impose their power on what is unfolding. Analogous to this process is a vase that, on receiving liquid, imposes a shape consistent with itself onto what has flowed in. Seen another way, this would be like a temperature of minus 10°F, which, when considered in the context of storing popsicles, would ensure that none of them melt and would be viewed as a good thing. On the other hand, when considered in the context of swimming for recreation, minus 10°F would be an impossible environment in which to do that. These archetypal, ideational abstractions are the behind-the-scenes determiners of that over which they have dominion. In the case of the first *yom* of Creation, that would be everything, transcendent of time and space.

FIRST CONCEIT

בְּרָא שִׁית (בְּרָאשִׁית) בְּרָא אלקים.

As discussed above, the dilemma here is the two-time occurrence of "He created" (בְּרָא). That these two references relate to creation *yeish me'ayin* certifies the simultaneity of their occurrence. That is, in spite of the appearance of some kind of a sequential set of conditions as a superficial read, there is and can only be one creation *yeish me'ayin*. This means that in some way, the creation *ex nihilo* of *shēt* (שִׁית) and *Elokim* (אלקים), (along with *shamayim* [שמים] *v'aretz* [וארץ]), are intertwined and dependent on each other for the sake of a world bounded by the forces inherent in duality.

Furthermore, and put another way, the flow of the first *yom* takes place, in general terms, as follows. God created, from absolute nihility, the ideational abstractions of the foundation of six (שִׁית), by using His attribute of *Elokim* (אלקים), simultaneously with the archetypes of heaven (שמים) and earth (ארץ). In addition, jumping the gun by one verse, with simultaneity, God also created the inner natures of *aretz*, *tohu* (תהו), and *bohu* (בהו) as abstractions. We'll have more on this critical understanding that God created *tohu* and *bohu*, *yeish me'ayin*, when we arrive at that verse.

ב

The oversized *bet* (ב) has the *gematria* of two. Taken in the context of the full verse, it signifies the announcement of the inception of the ideational abstraction of two-ness—the inherent, necessary, and sufficient state required for the advent of duality. Let's recall the citations in chapter 2 from Talmud *Yoma* 62b[8] and from Michael Alter's book,[9] and bring to mind the necessity of contrast (duality) for the sake of a multi-discrete world. As discussed at length in the overview, the distinction of distinctions is the ruler of the duality universe. This condition then determines all else that manifests, flowing from the first two *yamim* of Creation. The shape of the *bet*, almost like an open mouth in the act of speaking, opens toward the text that follows. This is a declaration that the first two *yamim* of Creation are the exposition of the unfolding of the nature of duality itself. This takes place through the power of the generative capacity of the normative, definitional, ideational abstraction of two; hence duality.

Further, although perhaps not quite so obvious at first, the letter *bet* is actually the first concerted "effort" on God's part in the genesis of Creation. As such, recalling the description from chapter 2, the power of this letter is the generative force in the creation of the *tzimtzum* and the *challal*. As said earlier, they are, in the abstract, the root of the primal singularity of the original black hole. Here, however, we also establish that the letter *bet* is the force that generates the original physical singularity itself. The primal black hole becomes itself when this abstraction comes into being. The *Zohar* reads:

> *When the most Mysterious wished to reveal Himself, He first produced a single point which was transmuted into a thought, and in this He executed innumerable designs, and engraved inummerable gravings. He further graved within the sacred and mystic lamp a mystic and most holy design, which was a wondrous edifice issuing from the midst of thought.*[10]

This is one of the *Zohar*'s representations of the most beginning of all beginnings.

---

8   Herzka, *The Gemara: Tractate Yoma*, vol. II, ch. 5, 62b[1].

9   Alter, *Why the Torah Begins with the Letter Beit*, p. 58, fn. 32

10   Harry Sperling, *The Zohar* (London: Soncino, 1931), vol. I, p. 6.

The *bet* also stands for *bein u'vein* (בין ובין) (literally, between and between), the power of differentiation and deduction. This is some of what Michael L. Munk says about the *bet* in *The Wisdom in the Hebrew Alphabet*. He goes on to say in reference to the nature of the *bet*, "R' Bunam of Peshisecha traces the root of אדם [Adam], man, to דמה, to compare. Man is characterized by his ability to compare and contrast, distinguish and differentiate, analyze and understand (*Otzar HaChaim*)."[11] This takes us back to the brief discussion from chapter 2 about the nature of Adam and Eve and their partaking of the Tree of the Knowledge of Good and Evil. The power of distinguishing distinctions belongs to God and was bestowed on us, as we are all *b'tzelem Elokim* (made in the image of *Elokim*).

ברא

The first word, *bara* (ברא): This verb is unique in the Hebrew language and belongs only to God, declaring that the nature of His creating is creation *ex nihilo*; the creation of something from absolute nihility; pure nothing-ness. Its reading in the text is "He created." We have two explicit statements of *bara* ("*Bara shēt bara Elokim et ha'shamayim v'et ha'aretz*"). However, in addition, according to the Ramban and Rabbeinu Bachya ben Asher, in their respective Torah commentaries, God created two primary materials from no-thing-ness. They both, along with an allusion from the Rambam to the term found in the *Moreh Nevuchim*, adopted the Greek term *hyule* (ὕλη) for the descriptor they attached to these materials. One *hyule* material is identified with heaven (שמים) and one *hyule* material is identified with earth (ארץ). *It is critical to think of these ideas as fundamental, archetypal, ideational abstractions that are opposite, interdependent, and complementary, and that have the power to generate all evolving manifestations that emanate from their interplay.*

For the stage of the unfoldment of the universe that's being referenced here, "material" is really a misleading term, as the two *hyule* are not physical or even vaguely physical at all. It must be understood that

---

11   Michael L. Munk, *The Wisdom in the Hebrew Alphabet* (Brooklyn: Mesorah, 1983), p. 66.

these materials are essential archetypal abstractions inhering in duality, which will then materialize as physical matter. Thus, as it says in the *Zohar*, "All of the spiritual universes are incapable of containing even one mustard seed."[12] It is also critical to recognize that the word *bara* is to be distinguished from verbs like *yatzar* (יצר) and *ya'as* (יעש), which mean various versions of "to make" or "to form" (using already existing created materials).

We know of two fundamental forces or (non-material) materials from the Chinese: *yin* (陰) and *yang* (陽). They are interpreted in exactly the same way as the term *hyule* is interpreted by the Ramban and Rabbeinu Bachya ben Asher. Looking "backward" toward the seeds of creation, the Chinese determined that the inherent structure of duality emanates from *yin* (陰) and *yang* (陽).

In the first verse of the Torah, *shamayim* (שמים) is seen by many Jewish Sages as a composite of *aish* (אש) (fire) and *mayim* (מים) (water). We must bear in mind that these are essential archetypes. In essence, they are ideational distinctions that are constituitive of the materialization of physical reality. They are not to be equated with actual physical water or fire or, for that matter, with heaven (outer space) or our planet. Commentators on these terms and ideas were mostly alluding to physical constructs; perhaps by doing so they were merely meaning to keep the deeper meanings hidden and unrevealed.

For example, the *Bahir* says that God "kneaded together fire and water to make *shamayim*." Obviously, no water like we swim in or fire that we find on a burning candle is what's being referred to in the *Bahir*. In simplest terms, that would create a logical absurdity and make utter nonsense out of the text. However, we have to sit up and take notice of the abstraction itself to really penetrate the meaning. Just to refresh the definitions so that the equations balance out, the Chinese character for *yin* represents the shady side of the hill and is the contractive, centralizing, condensing force (among other labels of description) of the universe and the Chinese character for *yang* represents the sunny side

---

12   Dovid Kamenetsky, *The Gemara: Tractate Chagigah* (Brooklyn: Mesorah, 1999), ch. 2, p. 14b, fn 23.

of the hill and is the expansive, distributing, dispersing force of the universe. They are complementary and opposite and mutually interdependent. They are the rock bottom, fundamental qualities (non-physical ones) of all multiplicity in the manifest and unmanifest world.

We can now take a moment to recapitulate the convergence of cross-cultural definitions. First, *hyule*, of which there are two "types." One is linked with heaven and *yang* and fire, (the position of above,) and light (and, as a preview, *tohu*). The other is linked with earth and *yin*, and water, (the position of below,) and darkness (and, of course, with *bohu*). In physical terms, we could use pairs of opposites like matter (*yin*) and energy (*yang*), inside (*yin*) and outside (*yang*), female (*yin*) and male (*yang*), cold (*yin*) and hot, (*yang*), etc. There is also a reference to the nature of above and below in Talmud *Chagigah*.[13]

In addition, from *Etz Chaim*, "Before all things were created…the supernal light was simple…When His simple will decided to create all universes…" And then from the *Zohar*, "At the head of the King's authority…and there emerged out of the Hidden of Hidden—the Mystery of the Infinite—an unformed line, embedded in a ring…"

The aim is to direct our attention to recognizing and clarifying the mystical and physical progression from unity to duality and on to the diverse manifestations of reality in the physical world.

שׁית

As discussed at some length earlier and just below in the context of the first phrase of the Torah, the word שׁית has two meanings that are relevant: "six" and "foundation." It is consistent with scriptural exegesis for both meanings to be operative singly, interchangeably and/or simultaneously. What we're going to establish is that the meaning here is sixness and foundation simultaneously. The fundamental notion is that the abstraction "six" is also foundational for all of Creation, along with the number two. The power of the number six is in essentially defining and designating space as having six physical directions. This is also described by the Maharal of Prague. *Shēt* (שׁית) is the object of the verb

---

13   Ibid., ch. 2, 12a, fn. 54.

bara, and is, in essence, an inherent property God used in the "process" of creating the universe. The *Zohar* and the *Bahir* describe the vacated space, the *challal*, that perfect sphere, as a necessity for the advent of the world. This three-dimensional space, defined by its six directions, is also the initial singularity, the original black hole which then expanded in the fireball of Creation.

The number six is embedded in the very design of many of the most fundamental physical structures upon which all known life depends. For example, the carbon atom contains six protons and is the sixth element by atomic number. Carbon and much of its chemistry is the basis of the discipline we call organic chemistry. Water in its solid form, ice, forms a six-sided hexagonal crystal structure, which we can see in the shape of snowflakes. Water in liquid form also displays a hexagonal formation through the power of what's known as hydrogen bonding. Carbon and water are the two absolutely essential ingredients required for life as we know it. This is certainly so on this planet of ours. NASA's Mars mission rover, Curiosity, scuttles around on the surface of our red sister planet, seeking evidence of water and carbon-based chemicals. The need for water for life to exist is obvious. What about carbon? Carbon is the element that forms the backbone of all organic chemicals. This category of chemicals is required for any form of life of which we know. This includes carbohydrates like sugars, and hydrocarbons like fossil fuels. No carbon, no life.

Carbon is the sixth element in the periodic table, as it is composed of six protons. No other element has six protons. Carbon bound to two oxygen atoms is carbon dioxide. We have a symbiotic relationship with plants that "breathe" in the carbon dioxide (CO_2) we breathe out and give us back oxygen for us to breathe in, in an ongoing cycle. A substance composed of six carbon atoms bound together in a ring, with each carbon atom bound to one hydrogen atom is the molecule known as benzene. Benzene is a chemical substance that is the primary feedstock in the synthesis of many more diverse and complex forms of organic compounds. Organic molecules and compounds are the basis for sugars, amino acids, proteins, hormones, neurotransmitters, DNA, RNA, enzymes, etc. The physical configuration of a spiral strand of

DNA displays certain geometric relationships. The geometry of a base, or base pair step, in the columnar structure of the double helix of DNA can be characterized by six coordinates: shift, slide, rise, tilt, roll, and twist. These values precisely define the location and orientation of every base or base pair in a nucleic acid molecule like DNA, relative to its predecessor along the axis of the helix. Together, they characterize the helical structure of the molecule. These molecules are required for life, and, especially, for complex forms of life.

The element of silicon is the main component of sand (silicon dioxide, SiO_2) and is second only to oxygen in abundance of all elements found in the earth's crust. Silicon is placed in the same chemical family as carbon, due to its atomic structure and it also has a hexagonal crystalline structure. Ultrapure silicon crystals are grown synthetically in order for semiconductor manufacturers to harvest silicon wafers from which computer microchips are produced. Pure silicon crystals have special electrical conductivity characteristics. The hexagonal nature of the crystal structure of silicon permits the electrical versatility necessary for the astounding process of producing semiconductors. The most complex engineering feats that have been accomplished by humankind have come as a result of the computational power provided by silicon.

All this takes place as a function of the properties of the semiconductor, providing for the electrical gates of the integrated circuit. In essence, the structure of six that is the crystal structure of silicon allows for the open or closed state of a semiconductor's governance over the flow of electricity. How astounding it is that the incredible complexity of computer capabilities rests on the simplicity of duality. That is, the conductive gate is either open or closed. The state is either yes or no, either the binary code is one or zero. The status is either *yin* or *yang*. Just like the human brain's computational power is endowed through the dual nature of the two hemispheres, so too is the silicon brain a binary phenomenon. So much power is unleashed through the power of the numbers two and six.

Have you ever looked at the structure of a honeycomb? Hexagons, little chambers of six-sided tubes all bunched together constitute the structure of the cells into which the bees deposit their honey. Certain other bees and wasps also produce hexagonal cells, even though there is no honey found there.

Question: Do you really think that bees know how to make perfect hexagons?! Profoundly, the answer is no, they don't. So where do the hexagons come from? What's going on? Why hexagons? If bees can't make hexagons and what we see are hexagons, how does that happen? The answer is that bees and wasps make circles, or actually circular (cylindrical) tubes. This is one of the marvelous manifestations of the *tzimtzum* in our world: the existence of the circle as a natural feature in the manifest world. When honeybees make their little cylindrical tubes of soft wax or paper wasps make their flimsy paper-like cells, they are making a series of many circular tubes that when squeezed together result in contiguous hexagonal tubes. If you can imagine the cardboard tube of a paper towel being squished together with many more tubes of the same diameter, such that where three of them meet and touch the space gets squeezed smaller and smaller until they disappear, what you'd have is an array of hexagonal tubes. Each set of six would be surrounding a central seventh.

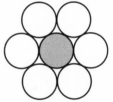

This property inherent in the nature of circular cylinders, spheres, and circles always produces six of one surrounding a central seventh of the same size, or, in the case of the bees, six hexagons surrounding a central seventh. But be clear that the bees and wasps are only making circular shapes. Six is the number that belongs inherently to the sphere and by extrapolation, to the circle. The sphere contains and defines the circle. The geometer's compass shows that circles of any size have an inherent relationship to circles of the same diameter that are just touching the circumference. That relationship is governed by the number six—six circles arranged around a central seventh. The same is true for spheres: in one plane of direction, six spheres surround a central seventh. Additionally, twelve spheres surround one sphere in three dimensions.

If you were to look inside an open, multicolored tulip flower, you would see a perfect hexagon at the bottom of the cup on the inside of the flower. If you were to longitudinally cut a cross section of a cucumber or zucchini and look at the cut end, you would see a perfect hexagon.

Try this experiment: Take a coin or a poker chip or a draftsman's compass and lay down one circle. Then align or draw circles of the exact same size just barely touching the first circle. You'll notice that you now have seven circles nestled together in perfect contiguity. This is comprised of a central circle surrounded by six identical circles. Now keep going. Place or draw circles of the same size as before in the gaps between each of the outer circles. You should now have added six more circles to make a total of thirteen circles in a perfectly configured "kiss" with those next to themselves.

Now, one more round. Place another gap-filling set of six circles in the appropriate places of the round of thirteen. Now, you see, you have a perfect **hexagon** made of nineteen circles in a tightly packed arrangement. That is, the sequence is one, seven (1 + 6), thirteen (7 + 6) or (1 + 12), and then nineteen (13 + 6) or (1 + 18) or (7 + 12).

Why does one circle generate the number nineteen? Here are a couple of answers. Nineteen is the number of fundamental particles in the quantum mechanical view of creation (at this writing). Not eighteen or twenty, but nineteen. Nineteen is also the number of years in the complete cycle of the Hebrew calendar. And, there are twelve non-leap years in that nineteen-year cycle. You can see that the number nineteen is generated from within the nature of the circle and the nature of the circle is tied to the number six and its multiples. "He created **six** (ברא שׁית)." We've now revealed the shaping forces imparted by the *tzimtzum*.

To further cement these facts into place, recall that there is an ancient phrase that clarifies the nature of six in Creation: "Last in deed but first in thought." This is the description given to the Sabbath. It took six *yamim* to get through to the Sabbath, but it was always the point above all else. Clearly, if the first phrase in the first verse of the Torah is *bara shēt*, we can see immediately that the Sabbath comes into existence at the very first with six-ness. The numbers six and seven are inextricably bound together in the physical world, and, therefore, we can recognize that they are yoked together in the abstract world of God's creating. We also find six words in **Shema** *Yisrael*, a fundamental profession of Jewish faith.

בְּרָא שִׁית

He created six. He created the foundation. He created the foundation of six. God created, from absolute nihility, the ideational abstraction(s) of the foundation of six (שִׁית). He created six-ness. This implies immediately, of course, that six-ness is, in fact, foundational to the creation of the entire universe. So what does six-ness signify? It signifies the *tzimtzum* and the initial black hole singularity. *Kabbalah* refers to *tzimtzum* as what God did in order to create the vacated space, the *challal*, into which to create the world. As described earlier, this is the spiritual void, a Divinely-specified ball-like hollow of perfect sphericity, whose characteristics include, or perhaps are made from, the six directions of three-dimensional space. This is seen in the X, Y, and Z axes of solid geometry and trigonometry and higher mathematic disciplines. These three axes (with two directions to each) encompass a three-dimensional space, regardless of

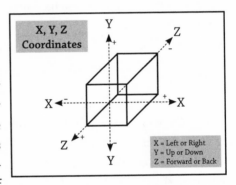

whether that space is a sphere, a cube, or whatever solid shape (in our time- and space-bound world) you may care to think about. *Bara shēt*: He created the foundation stone—the Shettiah Stone (שתייה or שתיה). This is the "place" (the location of the original singularity) from which the entire universe was founded and expanded. So, six generates the potential for solidity in our world. In the abstract, this is all happening within God's light and no physical form exists. Yet that potential is the abstraction, the ideational emblem of the three-dimensional reality in which we live. It correlates exactly with the advent of the original singularity of the first, primal black hole and the *bet* of *bara*.

בְּרָא

Even though as the Ramban has said, the order of the words in the first verse of the Torah implies a sequence, thereby relegating what is there to being a time-stream-generated narrative, this seems to be so and not so at the same time. As described above, *bara* cannot be ascribed any time-bound qualities. Therefore, the entire first verse and some matters beyond must be interpreted as a description of the simultaneously generated aspects of one whole creation. In describing the nature of this verse, any words I may use that seem to have time indicated in their meaning are used only as a convention for describing and not to actually mean anything about time. However, the first eight verses of Genesis are entering and exiting the timeless world of God's creating. Simultaneously, they are detailing the stages of the advent of and explosive expansion of the original singularity. In any case, the word *bara* has all of the same meanings in this location in the verse, and carries all of the same implications, as when we first encounter it at the head of the Torah.

אלקים

In discussing this word, we will be confining the discussion very narrowly. We're examining God's attribute of *Elokim* from the perspective of its most abstract nature as a Divine power. It is this power which operates exclusively throughout the entire first six *yamim* of Creation, and it is this attribute which is the pure, perfect architect of exactitude. Aryeh Kaplan, in his rendering of the *Sefer Yetzirah* (The Book of Formation), whose authorship is attributed widely to Abraham himself, says on page 7, "The name *Elokim*, which is used throughout the first chapter of Genesis, refers to the manifestation of delineation and definition." Of course, if one were to extrapolate from the abstract, spiritual-only dimension of *Elokim* into the world of human affairs, there are a natural set of distinctions that arise. We then find the following moral dichotomies: true/false, right/wrong, good/bad, responsible/irresponsible, and innocent/guilty, among others. Just as the exactitude in the world of abstractions works its way into our physical world, we should note that these moral parallels can appear self-evident within the context of the absolutism of *Elokim*. It should not be lost on us that in our currently everything-is-negotiable moral climate, the starkness of an absolute judge is anathema.

That said, the dimension, if you will, of *Elokim* that we're addressing here is not that which connotes unflinching judgment, *din*, in the human realm. What we are examining through the text does not bear on human behavior and the consequences of our human acts. Rather, it is the power above all powers of pure and perfect judgment, distinguishing "this" from "not-this," rigorously exact and precise in His "actions." This is the attribute that is the generator of contrast in our universe; the necessary and sufficient requirement for the creation of duality. However, it must be said strongly and clearly that *Elokim* itself is not dual in nature. It is that **out of which** the distinction of contrast, and, therefore, the distinction of distinction itself, comes. As said earlier, "At the outset, the creation of something out of 'everything—no-thing,' the drawing out of something from the field of all possibilities (creation *ex nihilo*, *yeish me'ayin*, something from nothing), rests on the capacity to distinguish distinctions."

Returning for a moment to the first words of the Torah, the power of *Elokim* must be being brought into existence simultaneously with the abstraction of the foundation of six, the *bet* at the head of the Torah, the original singularity, and heaven and earth. As difficult as it is to conceive, these two abstractions (the foundation of six and *Elokim*) are brought into existence simultaneously *ex nihilo*. In the *Zohar* (the Book of Enlightenment), the first verse of Genesis is referenced through the following narrative: "With the beginning, the Concealed One, Who is not known, created the palace. This palace is called *Elokim*. The secret is: With beginning, _____ created *Elokim*."[14]

While regarding the attribute of *Elokim* directly, I conclude, overviewing the entire first verse of the Torah, that the following is how to think about Creation so far: **While** [Hashem] is creating *Elokim* for the sake of the advent of the power of perfect differentiation, He is creating the foundation of six, **while** He is also creating heaven and earth: *Bara shēt bara Elokim et ha'shamayim v'et ha'aretz*—ברא שית [בראשית] ברא אלקים

---

14   Daniel Matt, *Zohar, the Book of Enlightenment* (New York: Paulist Press, 1983), p. 50.

את השמים ואת הארץ. Looking ahead a trifle, the archetypal nature of earth (*eretz*) is further detailed and differentiated within the first portion of the second verse: *V'ha'aretz haytah tohu va'vohu*—והארץ היתה תהו ובהו, which I'll deal with in great detail shortly. With the first verse, the state of existence of all of Creation is established *yeish me'ayin* and is necessary and sufficient for the making, *ya'as* (יעש) and the forming, *yotzar* (יצר), as distinct from creating *ex nihilo* of the world.

Were one to commission a brand-new home to be built for oneself, one would need a design and a location. Only after the site was prepared (usually by digging a hole in the ground—creating an empty space for the manifestation of the plans) would the implementation of the design begin. However, the design really needs to be complete before the digging begins, as one wouldn't know exactly where to dig without it. The architect of the design must be precise, exact, and perfect for the ideal execution of the plan to bring the design to life. Only after the design is approved, the empty space created, and the design implemented, does the construction yield a dwelling that is perfectly habitable for the purpose for which it was intended. This perfectly designed construction will not allow for habitation until it is complete. At that point, the inanimate house becomes a home for human life. Hopefully, the parallel is obvious here: only after the entire six *yamim* of Creation were complete, generated through the attribute of *Elokim*, could people come to inhabit the world. The perfect construction of the world required the attribute of *Elokim*, and solely *Elokim*. Hashem as Hashem, the Tetragrammaton, is not mentioned in the account of Creation, and I will maintain that the name Hashem wasn't "required" either. It was exclusively the perfectly ordered exactitude of the workings of the name *Elokim* that was needed for the universe to be created with the precision that was required for self-aware, free-will-endowed human beings to be able to be at home.

There is a certain property inherent in the very fabric of all of Creation. For example, it enables a rock to respond with an increase in its temperature as it is being bathed in direct sunlight. It makes the head of a sunflower turn and track the sun as it transits from east to west every day. Differences of temperature or light are the keys to these phenomena: each rests on a response to contrast. Cause and effect is one of its guises. One could say that all of these types of phenomena demonstrate the interrelatedness of opposites, of *yin* and *yang*. Within the framework of Chinese medical theory, there is a single functional and energetic capability which grants us the power of distinguishing distinctions. If, as we're maintaining, the distinguishing out of distinctions is a generating force in creating the universe (allied to and dependent on *Elokim*), the following description of this function will seem to be a natural fit. In order to elaborate on this understanding and gain further insight, we're going to reference a convergence of the perspectives of Chinese medicine and Western embryology. The capability that stems from the power of distinguishing distinctions we are referencing here in Chinese medicine is the power which generates and directs the differentiation of cells within a human embryo.

Once a human egg has been fertilized, that single cell begins to divide in an arithmetic progression: 1, 2, 4, 8, 16, 32, etc., doubling the number of total cells with each new division cycle. The embryonic disc is among the earliest of the named morphological stages in the development of the embryo, the stage in which minimal differentiation in cellular physiology or structure exists. However, at a certain point in the course of development after conception, what's called the primal node emerges. The primal node and the related primal streak that rapidly follows it are found along the building midline of the disc. The midline and its advent are the key to further normal development. Bilateral anatomical symmetry is the observable result of that. It is from these singular structural changes that the vast variety of cell types and structures then emerge on the way to becoming a human fetus and then a viable human being. The nature of these structures is that they initiate the separation into two distinct sides, whether named left and right or not, of the human body and brain. This mimics the creation of the distinction of distinctions in the beginning of God's creating of duality. The number two rules the tableau.

In Western medicine, an organ is composed of a physical tissue structure, in a particular location, with distinct histology and physiological function. However, within the system of Chinese medicine, what is termed to be an organ is a discrete energetic and functional capacity of influence. Further, this energetic and functional capacity is non-localized, not tied to a distinct physical location that comprises its whole existence. Chinese medicine is premised in a radically different paradigm of understanding of human existence than Western science. Western medicine views a human being as an ordered set of physical structures and chemical regulation, which has produced the epiphenomenon of consciousness. The core understanding of Chinese medicine is that a human being is, first above all, a conscious and self-aware spiritual being with a physically anchoring manifestation called a body. In Western medicine, different organs belong to different physicians and the body and mind are split into two distinct camps. Additionally, human spirituality has no place at all in the schema of Western medicine. However, Chinese medicine never posited any of those divisions and separations and thereby views each individual as one whole person, constituted of different, physically anchored interlocking and interdependent portions of one seamless, whole spiritual being.

What is this singularly unique functional and energetic capability about which Chinese medicine is speaking? It is the gall bladder. Now, from the perspective of Western medicine, the gall bladder is quite a minor player in the grand scheme of physical structures of things human. On a physical basis, it is dispensable and can be surgically removed with little or no fanfare, while leaving a virtually unaltered or minimally altered landscape of human function behind in its absence. However, using the Chinese medical approach, things are quite different. In chapter 8 of the oldest extant medical text in the world, the *Huang Di Nei Jing Su Wen*, commonly called *The Yellow Emperor's Inner Classic: Simple Questions*, the gall bladder is named and given the following description. It says that the gall bladder is "responsible for what is just and exact; determination and decision stem from it; the official of decision-making and wise judgment." As well, each of these main functions described in the Chinese medical classics has a "charge" or essential set of responsibilities. For the gall bladder, here is what it says:

The charge (guan) of the gall bladder is zhong zheng and has to do with squares and circles (round = heaven, square = earth): 1) Zhong represents an arrow hitting the center of a round target, hitting the bull's eye; this is the heavenly aspect—hitting the exact center; 2) Zheng is level and true and has to do with the making of correct 90 degree angles; it all has to do with exact and correct knowledge.

In addition, we can describe the Chinese character for the gall bladder (膽) as being made of three portions. The left-hand portion is what is known as the flesh radical (月). A radical in the system of Chinese characters is like a fundamental linguistic building block, and while radicals are sometimes found on their own, most often they are combined with other radicals and strokes to make a more complex character. Obviously, the more complex a character is, the more textured the interpretations of the character's meaning. In addition, meaning is commonly determined by the context in which the character is used. The upper right portion of the character for the gall bladder represents a person standing precariously on the top and edge of a high cliff, surveying the scene below in order to perceive and distinguish the distinctions of the landscape. A portion of the lower right half of the character includes the character for speech, indicating the capacity to speak the distinctions that are "perceived" into existence. The image indicates that reality will be generated by the very act of speaking the distinctions into existence. Prior to that speaking, however, is the attaching of linguistic labels to perceptions in one's mind. This, of course, is fully reminiscent of the position that I took earlier in the discussion about *Elokim*, which is summarized in this way:

Here we are examining God's attribute of Elokim, which is the pure, perfect architect of exactitude. What we are aiming to understand to a degree is the power above all powers of pure and perfect judgment, distinguishing "this" from "not-this," rigorously exact and precise in His "actions." This is the attribute that is the generator of contrast in our universe, the necessary and sufficient requirement for the creation of duality.

The precariousness of the position on the top of the cliff is only partially due to the physical position. The implied bulk of the danger in
such a situation is the peril inherent in appending linguistic markers
to the phenomenology of living. What this is saying is that, literally,
we create our reality by naming and labeling what we perceive through
our senses and the workings of our nervous systems. What we think
and say creates our experiential world and how we interact with it. The
conclusions that fall out from that fact, in summary form, are found in
appendix B, in a very brief synopsis from my book, *Abracadbra*, yet to
be published.

ברא אלקים

The power of creating "creating," the driver of duality, in being able to
spring into existence, "needs" the attribute of *Elokim* in order for itself
to become distinct. This is because the attribute that is the generator of
contrast (the epitome of distinctions) in our universe—the necessary
and sufficient requirement for the creation of duality—must, paradoxically, pre-exist creating "creating" for the abstraction of creating to come
into existence at all. Yet, equally paradoxically, creating creating is just
as "needed" by *Elokim* under the same conditions. As said earlier, "At
the outset, the creation of something out of "everything—no-thing,"
the drawing out of something from the field of all possibilities (creation
ex nihilo, yeish me'ayin, something from nothing) rests on the capacity
to distinguish distinctions." Thus, the essence of creating and *Elokim*
Himself must be at one with God Himself and co-exist as one. We must
constantly bear in mind that in this realm of the purely abstract, there
is no time. Simultaneity and co-existence is all there is in that realm.

Returning to the first words of the Torah, the attribute of *Elokim*
must be present, simultaneously, with the abstraction of the foundation of six for the sake of the existence of the universe. As difficult as it
is to conceive for us, these abstractions (creating "creating," the foundation of six, and *Elokim*) are brought into existence simultaneously
ex nihilo. In the *Zohar*, the Book of Enlightenment, referred to above,

the first verse of Genesis is referenced through the following narrative: "With the beginning, the Concealed One, Who is not known, **created the palace**. This palace is called *Elokim*. The secret is: With beginning, _____ created *Elokim*." (Please see the earlier citation of this translation on page 35.) All of the bold words are pointing in the direction of the simultaneity of Creation of all of the essential distinctions for the advent of a bounded world. All of the subjects of the verb *bara* are creations *ex nihilo* and arise together within the mysteries of the account of Creation. While regarding the attribute of *Elokim* directly, I conclude, overviewing the entire first verse of the Torah, that the following is how to think about Creation so far: **While** [God in His Essence] is creating *Elokim* for the sake of the advent of the power of perfect differentiation, He is creating the foundation of six, **while** He is creating heaven and earth: *Bara shēt bara Elokim et ha'shamayim v'et ha'aretz*—

בּרא שׁית [בּראשׁית] בּרא אלקים את השׁמים ואת הארץ.

CHAPTER FOUR

YOM ECHAD: FIRST VERSE, SECOND CONCEIT

ברא שית (בראשית) ברא אלקים את השמים ואת הארץ. והארץ היתה תהו ובהו וחשך על פני תהום ורוח אלקים מרחפת על פני המים. ויאמר אלקים יהי אור ויהי אור וירא אלקים את האור כי טוב ויבדל אלקים בין האור ובין החשך. ויקרא אלקים לאור יום ולחשך קרא לילה ויהי ערב ויהי בקר יום אחד.

SECOND CONCEIT

את השמים ואת הארץ.
Et ha'shamayim v'et ha'aretz—The heaven [the heavens, or heaven] and earth [the earth].

Keeping in mind that the first introduction of a word in the Torah establishes a definitional marker, we have to look very carefully at the new ideas being revealed in the second half of the first verse. Heaven and earth appear in the same verse as, yet immediately following, *Bara shēt bara Elokim*. Therefore, they are also a product of *bara*. The ideational abstractions of heaven and earth, introduced here for the first time, are the primal, archetypal emblems of the distinction of "opposite," both hidden and revealed, which are also created *ex nihilo*. In effect, then, the first verse could legitimately read: "He created the foundation of six, He created *Elokim*, He created heaven and earth." Interpolating, here's to where that brings us: "He created, *ex nihilo*, with simultaneity, the foundation of six, His attribute of *Elokim*, and the fundamental abstractions of opposites, heaven and earth." The *vav* (ו) that precedes the second *et* (את) between *shamayim* and *aretz* demands that we understand that the archetypes of heaven and earth are brought into existence **together** and are interdependently interlinked and intertwined with each other. Michael L. Munk says, "The letter *vav* is the prefix of conjunction; it unites manifold, even opposing, concepts. It is the link connecting heaven and earth." We will see this again when we examine *tohu va'vohu* (תהו ובהו) in the next verse. This is also true of the two *hyule*. Overarchingly, what stands up for forceful recognition in this second portion of the first verse is the consistent and insistent revelation of duality.

את

Et (את) is a unique word with intriguing implications. According to the Artscroll translation (and commentary) on the Ramban's Torah commentary, "The word *et* [is like the phrase] 'the essence of that thing,' [that is, that very thing itself.]" The Ramban goes on to say, "[The Sages] expounded this [word, asserting] that it always is [meant] to include [something extra not mentioned in the verse explicitly]." According to Rabbeinu Bachya ben Asher in his Torah commentary, "Whenever the word *et* (את) appears, it adds something to the meaning of the plain text. At the most basic level, the two words *et* here are meant to convey that two additional matters or raw materials were involved in the creation of heaven and earth."[15] This passage is referencing the two substance-less substances of Creation. The Greeks gave the label *hyule* (or *hylē*) (ὕλη), and the Ramban describes the advent of *hyule* this way: "[B]rought into being from complete, absolute nihility an exceedingly fine primary essence with no substance." Following, the Ramban says, "This is the primary substance called by the Greeks *hyule*. And after this *hyule*, [God] did not create (*bara*) anything." Finally, "You should know that heaven and all that is within are one substance, and earth

---

15   Bachya ben Asher, *Midrash Rabbeinu Bachya* (Jerusalem: Lambda, 2003), vol. I, p. 3.

and all that is within are one substance. The Holy One, Blessed is He, created both of these from nothing. These two things alone were created, and everything else is made from them. Now this substance is that which the Greeks called *hyule*." Therefore, two *hyule* are created, *ex nihilo*, a dual-natured essence-like substance (really, a substance-less substance), nothing about which is physical in the remote stretch of the imagination, and which is intimately and inextricably associated with heaven and earth: one paired entity. Furthermore, as the Ramban goes on to state, "God created [out of nothing] heaven, for He brought heaven's [primary] matter [*hyule*] into existence out of nothing, and earth, for He brought earth's [primary] matter [*hyule*] into existence out of nothing [as well]."

השמים

In order to understand this idea, I'll pull it apart and put it back together again. Our Sages have posited a few methods of seeing this word in two parts, thus encountering two words in this one word. While remembering that the frame of reference for this first verse is the beginning of the unfolding of duality, the question arises: Which two simpler words make up this single abstract archetype, given the context of its first appearance in the Torah? To my mind, there can be only one answer that fits coherently. In addition, that same answer satisfies the question: From whence did the water come, when we find the first discrete reference to it in the **second** verse? The answer lies in the *Bahir*, where it is said that "God kneaded together fire and water to make *shamayim*." This is saying that fire (*aish*, אש) and water (*mayim*, מים) essentially preceded the recorded acts of creation in the Torah. It says in the *Bahir*, according to Aryeh Kaplan, that "Rabbi Levatas ben Tavrus said: All agree, even Rabbi Yochanan, that the water already existed [on the first day]."

We can ask, therefore, what is the resultant of the kneading together of the archetypal fire and water? In a simple view, this would yield a liquid in a state of extremely high temperature. Given that they do not annihilate each other as physical fire and water would do, this merging must be producing something intrinsically necessary in the creation of

Creation. Theoretical physicists will recognize that a supremely hot liquid has put in an appearance in the manifestation of the universe. As we will discuss at some length in chapter 7, the temperature of the rapidly expanding fireball (a plasma) which emerged from the initial black hole, was estimated in its first moments to have been dramatically higher than 10^{32} degrees Kelvin (10 with 32 zeroes following it). Zero degrees Kelvin is called absolute zero and is approximately 459.67 degrees below zero, Fahrenheit. It had the property of being a "near-perfect" liquid. It manifests here, at the outset, in the formless, virtually massless, virtually infinitely hot, virtually perfect liquid (i.e., with almost no viscosity) that comprises the plasma at the first instants of the Big Bang.

Switching perspectives for a moment to a Chinese one, the abstractions of water (水) and fire (火) are also archetypes corresponding with *yin* (陰) and *yang* (陽), respectively. Keep in mind that the Chinese character for *yin* represents the shady side of the hill and is the contractive, centralizing, concretizing force (among other labels of description) of the universe, and the Chinese character for *yang* represents the sunny side of the hill and is the expansive, distributing, organizing force of the universe. They are opposite and complementary and mutually interdependent. For example, the air on the shady side of a hill sinks, has higher density and, of course, is much colder than its opposite-hillside companion. The air on the sunny side of a hill rises up, is less dense and is warmer. The Chinese hold that *yin* and *yang* are the fundamental inherent natures (non-physical ones) of all multiplicity in the manifest and non-manifest world. Without regard to from which language all of these terms come, or from which ancient source or culture, we must bear in mind that these concepts are held as essential archetypes: quintessential poles in the dance of duality. Aryeh Kaplan says, in *Innerspace*, "God created *chokhmah-abba* and *binah-ima* [two *sefirot* from *Kabbalah*]. These are the masculine and feminine forces of creation.......They may be two separate *partzufim* [archetypal personas] but they never manifest in exclusion to each other." We will see a similar dual nature within earth in the second verse when we discuss *tohu va'vohu*.

The water and fire we are referencing should not be equated with physical water or fire or, for that matter, should heaven be equated with outer space or earth with our planet. Therefore, and as such, we need to take these primary terms as ideational templates that function as archetypes of shaping. Were it to be that they referred to physical states, it would trivialize the majesty of the text. However, the properties of physical fire and water are congruent indicators of the qualities of the archetypal energies from which they derive their existence. Fire rises, disperses, and animates. Water descends, coheres, and stills. The primal, archetypal forces are then proceeding to the gradual and complete manifestation of physical-ness as their final destination.

Our Sages seem to have conformed to a more mundane interpretation of these esoteric verses so as to hew to the dictum of not revealing or clarifying the mystical interpretations too deeply. For example, juxtapose how we regard the sky above that we see with our physical eyes, versus *shamayim*, in its most abstract, mystical construction. While both are called *shamayim*, failing to differentiate the "levels" can generate a very blurry understanding of the text. This can lead to confusion. My aim is to clarify the mystical as much as I can through the abilities and perspectives that I have at my command. Perhaps through this discussion, we have shown the converging archetypal pairs across cultures: heaven and earth, fire and water, *yang* and *yin*, and the two paired *hyule*.

את השמים

We've already discussed the word *et* (את) at some length. In this case, it points out that much more is behind the simple meaning of the word *shamayim*. Secreted within heaven (שמים) are the two fundamental abstractions of fire (אש) and water (מים).

ואת

The *vav* in *v'et* tells us that *shamayim* and *aretz* are wedded to each other and are inseparable. This is equivalent to *yin* and *yang*, whose intertwining we find exemplified by the familiar symbol. It also declares that there is more to *aretz* than the simple meaning. Its hidden aspects are about to be revealed. This is congruent with what was made clear about *shamayim*. In short, the *vav* joins *shamayim* and *aretz* with each other, declaring that they are yoked to each other inseparably, particularly through their deeper meanings. In addition, as with the *et* that is associated with *shamayim*, the *et* here is declaring that there is much yet to be revealed about earth. Fortunately, what is to be brought to light follows right behind in the second verse.

הארץ

This is not the earth upon which one stands or sits, nor walks. It's not even the earth whose picture from space sent back from our astronaut explorers engenders within us a sense of awe for Creation. No, this earth does not exist in any familiar physical form. Additionally, the ancient notion of explicating *aretz* as being comprised of the four elements is a departure from an abstract mystical understanding. The four-element representation doesn't provide illumination for the sake of penetrating the meaning of the archetypal *aretz* on an **abstract** level. So, I am going to leave aside commenting on the Greek notion of the four elements that has been employed by others to describe the properties of earth.

As said earlier, when a word first appears in the Torah, it has the property of being a prototypical emblem of abstract ideational power. Of course, by virtue of its appearance in the first verse and its position there, earth is necessarily defined as a function of its paired status with heaven. Many commentators, particularly the Kabbalists, speak of heaven as male and earth as female. This includes the fact that the word *aretz* is a feminine noun. In common speech, we also say that our Father is in Heaven and that this is Mother Earth. There are many more examples of this gender designation throughout scriptural commentary, as well as cultural literature.

We are going to take the gender association as an allusion, indicating that earth is like the mother who makes physical form within her. The essential features of these descriptions are that they indicate a link to the direct progenitor of form—not being actual form yet, but as an archetype and precursor, or proto-matter. That is, it is the *capacity* to produce form and substance. In addition, a mother produces substance *within* herself, and the potential for this capacity comes as a function of the interiorizing and materializing power that is an inherent feature of earth. In this way, we come to see this *aretz* as the seed of all potential for condensing materialization of the entire universe, including matter and energy, manifesting the world.

In the Artscroll *Tanach* Series, a short elucidation of *aretz* appears attributed to Ibn Caspi.[16] Ibn Caspi was Yosef ben Abba Meir ben Yosef ben Yaakov Caspi (1280–1345) of Largentière, in current-day France. Ibn Caspi, although not widely known, was a prolific scriptural commentator of his time. Titles of his works include *Matzref le-Kesef* (Crucible for Silver) and *Tirat Kesef* (Palace of Silver). Many of his titles include the word silver. His name, Caspi, means "of silver." This is the comment on *aretz* attributed to him: "It (*aretz*) is also derived from *ratzatz* (רצץ), meaning "that which is compressed." He seems to have grasped the essence of *aretz* as befits the archetypal abstractions I am describing in this work. As described above in multiple ways, the nature of the Chinese term *yin* is that it is a density-making force; one that is an expression of centripetal forces, producing condensation and compression. Ibn Caspi put his finger right on the abstraction by his determination that the *shoresh* (root) of *aretz* (ארץ) is *ratzatz* (רצץ). This is consistent with the understanding provided by the pairing of earth with heaven in the first verse and with *yin* in the classical understanding from the Chinese.

Amongst our more noted scriptural commentators, the Ramban, in particular, discusses what was considered to be the essential mystical nature of earth found in the first verse of Genesis. In Genesis 1:8, the Ramban discusses the distinction of *shamayim* being the primordial heaven, which, of course, means that the *aretz* is primordial as well. Additionally, I have found relevant commentaries on this *aretz* by the Ramban and Rabbeinu Bachya ben Asher, but not in *Parashat Bereishit*. Surprisingly, we refer to another *parashah*, in a completely different section of the Bible. In the case I am citing, we need to look all the way to *Parashat Ha'azinu*, in the book of Deuteronomy.

---

16 Meir Zlotowitz, *The Artscroll Tanach Series Bereishis/Genesis* (Brooklyn: Mesorah, 1986), section I, p. 34.

Just as the first scriptural mention of *aretz* (ארץ) in the Torah is in the first verse of Genesis, this elucidation of it as an archetype is found in the first verse of *Ha'azinu*. The Ramban and Rabbeinu Bachya ben Asher similarly discuss *aretz* in *Ha'azinu*: *Ha'azinu ha'shamayim v'ad-abeira v'tishma ha'aretz imrei phee*—האזינו השמים ואדברה ותשמע הארץ אמרי פי. When Moses is calling on heaven and earth to bear witness to the covenant with the children of Israel, he is asking for the "eternal" heaven and earth to do so. From Rabbeinu Bachya: "The words *shamay-im va'aretz* of which Moses speaks here are...in the very first verse of Genesis...Moses did not address the phenomena visible to the human eye such as sky and earth, but to the mystical elements they represent and that are the elements with which the Jewish people entered into a covenant." The Ramban says, "And by way of the Truth [the mystic teachings of the *Kabbalah*], the reference here is to the first [higher] heavens and earth mentioned in Genesis, for it is they that shall enter the covenant with Israel."

The essence of this passage, seen through the eyes of our Sages, is that only the archetypal heaven and earth are eternal and are recognized as such, as they are referenced in the first verse of Genesis. This eternality is such as a function of heaven and earth being fundamental ideational emblems—archetypes of the powers of duality. One would think here that *aretz* (ארץ), just like *shamayim* (שמים), should also now show a dual inner nature. But that is not immediately apparent from the word alone. No reference can be teased out of the word itself, nor from any analysis of its letters or their order. So, the clarity of what is meant by earth in this context is most definitively given to us by Ibn Caspi, contextually illuminated by the Ramban and Rabbeinu Bachya ben Asher. This sets the stage for the exposition provided in the second verse. The mystery of *aretz* isn't fully uncovered until we find the power hidden within the oft-misunderstood terms, *tohu va'vohu*.

ואת הארץ—V'ET HA'ARETZ

As mentioned before, the *vav* in *v'et* tells us that *shamayim* and *aretz* are wedded to each other and are inseparable. The *vav* links the pow-er of both *et* and *aretz* in this instance, as it demands that the earth archetype never be considered separately from heaven. The *et* belonging to *et ha'shamayim* and the *et* of *v'et ha'aretz* both point us in the direction of what is additionally so, but not made explicit in the verse itself. Together, they comprise the two fundamental archetypes of the contrast spoken of in *Talmud Yoma* 62b as the source of all multiplicity. This, along with the mystical reference to the eternality of their natures from *Parashat Ha'azinu*, allows us to recognize that their inner essences are fundamental keys to Creation. This view is parallel to that afforded by our understanding of *yin* and *yang*, whose intertwined relationship is an essential ground of being for all of creation. As we see from the familiar symbol signifying the unity of *yin* and *yang*, the contrasting yet complementary two-ness of *yin* and *yang* inheres in the whole. This is congruent with what was revealed about *shamayim*. In short, the *vav* relates *shamayim* and *aretz* with each other, declaring that they are yoked to each other, particularly through their deeper, archetypal meanings. Fortunately, what is to be brought to light about earth follows right behind in the second verse. The hidden aspects of *aretz* are about to be revealed.

If we look to *shamayim* by itself, we find *aish* (אֵשׁ—fire) and *mayim* (מִים—water) "inside," as dual constituents. This serves as a model for our investigation. Since we are in the realm of the unfolding of duality, we're really looking for dual-natured, intertwined, complementary yet interdependent abstract ideational emblems. In the first verse, we have encountered heaven and earth and fire and water. By implication from the verb *bara*, we have also found Creator and created. We have also discovered three-dimensional space through the nature of the *tzimtzum* and, of course, its interwoven counterpart, time. Albert Einstein gave us certitude about this dual-natured pair. Lastly, we have *Elokim*, the perfect Judge and His distinction of distinctions: God's attribute that relates to contrast.

Throughout the first two *yamim*, we find polar opposites abounding, light and darkness, *yom* and *laylah*, *mayim* above the *rakiya* and *mayim* below the *rakiya*. There is also the inference of opposites by virtue of the language surrounding such terms as *b'toch* (בְּתוֹךְ), *mavdil* (מַבְדִּיל), *bein* (בֵּין), etc. Lastly, to particularize, there is the yet-to-come *tohu* and *bohu.* In the final analysis, however, we have heaven above and earth below, just as we say at the end of the first paragraph of *Aleinu*, at the conclusion of the Jewish prayer services. The implications that we can draw from this fundamental contrast—and what is also implied by all of the other contrasting pairs in the first two *yamim* of Creation—is that the duality that God sought by virtue of His simple will through the advent of the *tzimtzum* is clearly here for all of us to see and live with, in our own dual existence: with a body and a soul and a *yetzer tov* (a good inclination) and a *yetzer hara* (its opposite, an evil inclination) as our own dual constituencies. All, we will see, is for our benefit and is necessary for our progression along the path of our own becoming.

CHAPTER FIVE

YOM ECHAD: SECOND VERSE, FIRST CONCEIT

ברא שית (בראשית) ברא אלקים את השמים ואת הארץ.
והארץ היתה תהו ובהו וחשך על פני תהום ורוח אלקים
מרחפת על פני המים. ויאמר אלקים יהי אור ויהי אור. וירא
אלקים את האור כי טוב ויבדל אלקים בין האור ובין החשך.
ויקרא אלקים לאור יום ולחשך קרא לילה ויהי ערב ויהי בקר
יום אחד.

SECOND VERSE

והארץ היתה תהו ובהו וחשך על פני תהום ורוח אלקים
מרחפת על פני המים.

In my reading of this verse, the following seems to be the most illu-minating translation: "And the earth was (conceived of) lines of *tohu* and stones of *bohu*, and darkness (was) on the face of the deep, and the spirit of *Elokim* hovering upon the surface of the water."

Of course, we can employ many authoritative English translations that differ to greater or lesser degrees, but the above seems to be the most salient choice for our particular frame of reference. I have left *tohu* and *bohu* untranslated for the moment, in order to highlight the construction and context of this verse before getting to the meaning of these two mystical terms.

Once again, the *vav* with which this verse begins demands high attention. It links and continues the first verse, and although the first
and second verses are apparently distinct from each other, they read
like they are one single construction. The first *vav* of the second verse
dictates that this is so. Actually, a *vav* appears in this verse four times,
linking each sub-phrase to the other sub-phrases and linking them all
back to the first verse together. The language we are applying to *tohu*
and *bohu* comes to us from Isaiah 34:11, and the context we are using
within which to understand them is taken largely from the Ramban's
commentary on *Bereishit*, along with my understanding of *yin* and *yang*.

Particularly of interest as well is the verb *haytah* (היתה). While seeming to be innocuous enough, this word has been a source of befuddle-
ment. On the one hand, it seems obvious that this means "was" (or "had
been," if this is the pluperfect tense, as it says in a footnote comment to
this passage in *Torah Sheleimah*[17]), as if the tense of it describes a former
state that had been left behind. However, I'm taking the position that
this is misleading and contextually incorrect.

על פני

Further along in this verse, the construction *al pnei* (על פני) appears
a second time, and by a rule of standard Torah exegesis that states that
similar words in different contexts are meant to clarify one another,
this establishes that each is related to the other. We will explore this in
depth with the assistance of our Sages' commentaries, with supporting
evidence from current thinking in modern theoretical physics.

FIRST CONCEIT

והארץ היתה תהו ובהו.

I want to continue the text from the first verse, as if it's one extended sentence: "He created the foundation of six, He created *Elokim*,
[and] heaven and earth, and the earth was *tohu* and *bohu*." What's

---

17   Menahem M. Kasher, *Encyclopedia of Biblical Interpretation* (New York: American Biblical
Encyclopedia Society, 1953), vol. I, p. 17, fn. 67.

happening here is the elaboration and extension of the revelation of duality. Clearly, however, the Torah is now describing expanded details about the inner nature of the precipitation of duality into the world. As we move further along through the text, we begin to see the emergence of the world we think of as our own. In another footnote from *Torah Sheleimah*, when speaking about תהו ובהו we find the following: "God first created *tohu* and *bohu*, these being very fine substances, and out of these He created the world." This is precisely the same language as the Ramban's comments on the *hyule* (ὕλη), of which we spoke at length earlier and, of course, *yin* and *yang*.

The two *hyule* are the archetypal substance-less substances of the abstraction "opposites," which could simply be named *yin* and *yang*, as well as heaven and earth, from the first verse of Genesis. Whatever the case, *tohu* and *bohu* each and together have a simultaneously generated, interdependent, complementary co-existence, linked together with a *vav*, yoked to each other inseparably. Accepting this perspective, it becomes clear that *tohu* does not change or transform into *bohu* as time moves forward or as any staging or sequence moves along, nor could it. Furthermore, as Aryeh Kaplan says:

> *This process is actually taking place in a conceptual or logical time dimension. By analogy, if you prove a geometrical theorem, you go from step 1 to step 2 to step 3. The proof is thus unfolding in time. Yet, it is totally independent of time. The same is true of these kabbalistic processes. Because our minds are time oriented, we see them unfolding in time. Actually, they proceed in a logical sequence that is totally independent of time.*[18]

Tohu and *bohu* are each distinct from, and complementary to, each other, and each is necessary for the existence of the other. This is identical to the natures of the primeval *aish* and *mayim*, the two *hyule*, the eternal heaven and earth and *yang* and *yin*. Notwithstanding certain

---

18   Kaplan, *Innerspace*, p. 204, fn. 8.

other perspectives, from a mystical, abstract, archetypal perspective, time is poised to flow at this stage in the Creation narrative. The narrative just here is a descriptive rendering of the barest onset of a progressive movement or sequence of things in mere fractions of time. For all intents and purposes, and certainly on a physical basis, nothing has really happened yet. The universe is about to come into existence, but it is too soon to say anything concretely about what or how it is.

והארץ

This is not our planet, nor any other planet. This is the archetypal epitome of the concretizing potential of the whole of the created world. The succeeding word pair, *tohu va'vohu*, provides us with the explication of the dual **inner detail** of *ha'aretz*. This is so just as *aish* and *mayim* detail the dual inner nature of *shamayim*. Thus, the symmetry demanded by the paired features of duality is invoked and satisfied with this first portion of the second verse. In the case of *shamayim*, the dual nature is found inside the word itself, indicating to us that the inner nature of heaven is more non-manifest and ethereal (*yang*). In the case of *aretz*, with its inner duality exposed through the use of the externalized words, *tohu* and *bohu*, it is more concretely displayed, formed, and evident, consistent with the nature of the more densely manifesting aspect of the world (*yin*). This exposition is clearly based on the logic of the *yin/yang* pair. That is, *yin* is contractive, centralizing, and condensing, and *yang* is expansive, distributing, and dispersing.

היתה

When we read the first *yom*'s text, it is apparent that what is being described is an unfolding of some sort, sequenced in some kind of framing like the flow of time. When we encounter a Hebrew word written in the past tense, the natural inclination is to relate to the text as if there is a time sequence being reported with contrasting "positions" at $time_0$, $time_1$, $time_2$, etc. Emphatically, however, the position we are establishing is that this is not the case here. I ask you to bear in mind that we are now calling on the use of *haytah* (היתה) to direct us to encounter a statement of a conceptual state, instead of a statement referencing time. Once we settle into the idea that the use of היתה is solely readying us for a statement of characterization, we can explore the nature of *tohu* and *bohu* as if this is a case of magnification, trained on the mystical nature and meaning of "earth."

As an example of this assertion about a statement of state, if one were to give an account of meeting someone, one must use descriptors: while describing someone's appearance, one might easily say, "He was skinny and tall." However, this way of speaking doesn't mean that we are measuring his height or weight *now* and comparing the two observations. Rather, it is a characterization, not a detail determined because of a time reference. As well, I am saying here that the use of היתה is solely a vehicle for characterization, or, better said, an elaboration, of the inner, mystical nature of earth. To emphasize, and at the risk of belaboring the point, we must bear in mind that Creation only seems to be able to be characterized as being in the past, since we are inured to living as if the forward flow of time is the only reality. However, this is not so from God's perspective, as everything is **now**, nor is it so from a mystical perspective. Past, present, and future are all one. The account of Creation **is**. We could fairly say that this is so from microsecond to microsecond, and that that is all there is. From a mystical point of view, Creation is not some past event that had a beginning, which we are only now apprehending. That it could be viewed as a past occurrence is due entirely to the way sensory input is processed through the human nervous system, reinforcing the gripping illusion (*sheker*) that we are time- and space-bound beings. The *Midrash Rabbah* on *Bereishit* says, "[W]hereas the first half of the verse speaks in the past tense [*hay-tah*—היתה], this phrase [*merachephet al ha'mayim*—מרחפת על פני המים] uses the present tense."[19]

In *Inner Space*, Aryeh Kaplan says,

> [T]he psalmist says, "Forever, O God, Your word stands in the heavens (Psalm 119:89). The Baal Shem Tov explains that

---

19   Yaakov Blinder, *Sefer Bereishis: The Midrash: Midrash Rabbah* (Brooklyn: Mesorah, 2014) vol. I, ch. 2, p. 5, fn. 44.

"Your word" refers to the saying, "God said, 'There shall be a fir-mament in the midst of the waters'" (Genesis 1:6). The words and letters of this saying stand and remain forever within the firmament of the heavens, giving them existence. If they would be removed, even for an instant, everything would revert to nothingness.

Looking at another saying, the Torah writes, "God said, 'There shall be light,' and there was light. And God saw the light that it was good" (Genesis 1:3). In this instance as well, we see God literally speaking the physical universe into existence.[20]

In our morning prayers, we say that He (God) "renews [present tense!] daily, perpetually, the work of Creation (*Ma'aseh Bereishit*)." God created the world within His own eternality, in "non-time." The present tense status of "renews" and "perpetually" tells us that the creation of the world is not bounded by time. Therefore, the creation of Creation is an eternal act, and without that eternality, all of Creation would "revert to nothingness." When we say that God "looked" into the Torah to create Creation, we are stating that there is design in it and that God is using the Torah as a builder would use an architect's renderings. When God is in the act of "speaking," the Creation which we encounter in the first chapter of Genesis is the account of Creation. In Talmud *Chagigah* 11b, it states that the opening passages of the Torah comprise *Ma'aseh Bereishit*, the account of Creation.[21] Particularly, in footnote 33 it says, "Literally, *Ma'aseh Bereishit* means account of Creation." And, slightly further along in the same footnote, "*Ma'aseh Bereishit* pertains to the account of the world's creation recorded in the first chapter of Genesis…" The first chapter carries through to the end of the sixth *yom*.

So, now let us read that portion of our morning blessings as, "He renews daily, perpetually, the **account** of Creation" (my emphasis). The meaning of this is that the letters and their arrangement in the first chapter of the Torah are the account of Creation and that God uses

---

20   P. 114.
21   Kamenetsky, *The Gemara: Tractate Chagigah*, ch. 2, p. 11b, fn. 3 and 33.

those letters to create Creation as an ongoing enterprise, in spite of its appearance to us as a series of events lodged in the ancient past. With this idea clearly in mind, the word *haytah* stands out for interpretation as a characterization of state only. Despite its tense being in the past construction, it must be eternal. The logic is sound for this conclusion. There's more to be said on this in chapter 7. Speculatively, however, its past tense construction is for the sake of an interpretation that fits the common-sense understanding that, surely, Creation must have taken place in the past. This would satisfy the non-mystical *p'shat* (face value or simple) rendition of the beginning of the Torah. In any case, and in summation, what we are finding here in reference to *haytah* is a statement of present, conceptual, or logical time, and not, to be sure, a record of chronology or sequence in time.

תהו

To capture the essence of what the Torah is saying here we have to re-capitulate some fundamental ideas. God brought forth, simultaneously, from absolute nihility, two primary substances, both of which our Sages called by the Greek name *hyule* (ὕλη). Here's how the Ramban recounts this: "You should know that the heavens and all that is in them are one substance and the land (*aretz*) and all that is in it are one substance. The Holy One, Blessed is He, created (ברא) both of these from nothing. These two things alone were created (*ex nihilo*), and everything else is made (נעשים) from them." The next sentence from the Ramban in this sequence makes it very difficult to understand the mystical nature of *tohu* and *bohu*, particularly in relation to the two *hyule* that were created *ex nihilo*. This is what he goes on to say: "Now this substance, which the Greeks called *hyule*, is called *tohu* in the Holy Tongue." This presents a confusing difficulty, because there are **two** *hyule*, and, therefore, logical-ly each can't have the same name as the other, as they are of an opposite yet complementary polarity to each other.

The inner natures of the two *hyule*, which belong to those of *shamayim* and *aretz*, when juxtaposed with *tohu* and *bohu*, respectively, are congruent when viewed from the perspective of *yin* and *yang*. That is, as said earlier, heaven is a configuring and expansive force, while earth is a concretizing and contractive force. These are emblematic abstractions that carry the exact same natures as do *yang* and *yin*, respectively. However, we must bear in mind that the two *hyule* are the only "things" that were created *ex nihilo*. In order for me to further clarify the nature of these two *hyule*, I again cite the Ramban: "God created out of nothing the heavens, for He brought their primary matter (*hyule*) into existence out of nothing, and the earth, for He brought its primary matter (*hyule*) into existence out of nothing as well." These **two** (my emphasis) primary substances (really, substance-less substances) were inseparably born *ex nihilo* **together**; paired and interdependent. Were it to be the case that *hyule* = *tohu*, then we are left with the two *hyule*, each of which, or together, are called *tohu*. That leaves a serious problem in the pairings, the essential structure of the first two days. First, are there two *hyule* brought into existence simultaneously, *ex nihilo*, and each (both? together?) are called *tohu*? That leaves *bohu* floating off independently and without a partner. Given that the structure of the language is *tohu va'vohu*, and the context is that of the unfolding of duality, this is unacceptable.

Menachem Kasher cites Rabbi Shimon bar Yochai:

> *I am astonished that these great teachers debated the matter at all [whether earth preceded heaven or heaven preceded earth]; surely both heaven and the earth were forged simultaneously like a pot with its lid (which are made simultaneously in the same mold)...Rabbi Eliezer bar Rabbi Shimon commented: "My father's opinion explains why Scripture sometimes gives precedence to the earth over the heaven, and at others the reverse, which teaches that they are equals."[22]*

Let's revisit the discussion about *shamayim* and *aretz* written earlier on in the first verse, by repeating a portion of what was written there:

> *The vav (ו) that precedes the second et (את) between shamayim and aretz demands that we understand that the archetypes of*

---

22   Kasher, *Encyclopedia of Biblical Interpretation*, vol. I, p. 13, fn. 51.

> *heaven and earth are brought into existence* **together** *and are interdependently interlinked and intertwined with each other. We will see this again when we examine tohu va'vohu (תהו ובהו) in the next verse. Overarchingly, what stands up for forceful recognition in this second portion of the first verse is the consistently insistent revelation of duality.*

It would be impossible, as was discussed while explicating the first verse, for a chronology or a sequence to be implicated, much less made explicit, as long as the verb *bara* is operating. Therefore, since one of these two *hyule* corresponds with *shamayim* and one with *aretz*, it is clear that they come into existence simultaneously and one cannot change, transform, or become the other while under the dominion of *bara*. Unfortunately, this flies in the face of the Ramban's statement about *hyule* being equivalent to *tohu*, made just a sentence or so before, given that there are **two** *hyule*, each having an inherently different inner nature, where inner natures demand two different names.

In Isaiah 34:11, it says the following: "*V'natah aleha kav tohu v'avnei vohu*—ונטה עליה קו תהו ואבני בהו." Here is what the Ramban writes about this: "This is what Scripture says, 'He will stretch out over it a rope-line of *tohu* (קו תהו) and stones of *bohu*. For the rope-line (is that) with which the builder outlines his building plan and what he hopes to accomplish." The *Tanach* translation is, "He will draw against it a line of *tohu* and plumb bobs of *bohu*."[23] The footnote from the *Tanach* says, "The line and the plumb bob are builders' tools used to ensure the horizontality (*yin*) and verticality (*yang*) of layers of stones or bricks." The footnotes from the Ramban say, "The lines are called 'lines of *tohu*' because they are used for planning, and not in the actual building process. They represent the potential, as opposed to the actual." And, "The stones are called 'stones of *bohu*' because, as opposed to the rope-line, they are used in the actual building."

In both instances, in Isaiah itself and in the Ramban's commentary, we find the coupling of the word for line (*kav*—קו) with the use of the word

---

23   Scherman, *Tanach: The Stone Edition*, p. 1011, ch. 34, v. 11.

tohu. In the early portion of the nineteenth psalm, it says, "The heavens declare the glory of God, and the expanse of the sky [actually, *rakiya*—הרקיע; more on this in the portion on *yom sheini*] tells of His handiwork. Day following day brings expressions of praise, and night following night bespeaks wisdom. There is no speech and there are no words; their sound is unheard. Their line (קום) goes forth throughout the earth..."[24] The last two sentences read, "אין אמר ואין דברים, בלי נשמע קולם. בכל הארץ יצא קום—*Ein omer v'ein d'varim, b'li nishma kolam. B'chol ha'aretz yatza kavam.*" The root of the word קום is *kav* (קו) and the footnote to this passage says the following, "*Their line.* The precision of the universe is likened metaphorically to a surveyor's tape (*tohu*) stretched out to the ends of the earth. This means that the precision of the cosmos is evident all over the earth to any observer." Now let us bring back the imagery from the discussion on *Elokim*, written earlier and repeated here: "Here we are examining God's attribute of *Elokim* from the perspective of its most abstract nature as a Divine power. It is this power which operates exclusively throughout the entire first six days of Creation and **it is this attribute which is the pure, perfect architect of exactitude.**"

In order to tease this apart further, we have to determine the meaning of the words in the context of the psalm. First, whose possessive relationship is being referenced by the use of the word "their" at the very beginning of this passage, as in "their line"? From the context at the beginning of the psalm, it appears to be the heavens, making the beginning of this portion read "heavens' line..." Second, through which earth is the heavens' line going throughout? As this appears to be a description relating to a primordial ordering of the universe, the earth that's being referenced here is the earth of the very first verse of the Torah. That is, this is the earth which is the archetypal abstraction having to do with the potential for **manifestation** of a physical world. One could reasonably think of this as being congruent with the proto-matter and proto-energy of the primordial cosmic fireball of the Big Bang.

Surveyors' lines are lines of organizational exactitude. For the

---

24   Nosson Scherman, *The Artscroll Siddur* (Brooklyn: Mesorah, 1987), p. 374–5, fn.

architect, plans alone are not enough. There has to be a mechanism which can generate order for the sake of the implementation of those plans and there has to be systematic organization for the plans to be executed properly. Taking my cue from the abstractions discussed from the first verse's presentation of *Elokim*, *tohu* is the actively organizing, configurative force, determining and upholding the ordering of the manifestation of the Architect's plans for the sake of manifesting the world. The nature of this description places it at the extreme *yang* end of the scale from *yin* to *yang*. Recalling the basis of the discussion about *yin* and *yang* from earlier, the complementary opposites relevant in this discussion are active and structive. Structive is a bit of an odd word, but it comes from the Latin verb *struere* (pronounced strew-air'-ee), which means to build. So, the forces of active organization are *yang*. In complementary fashion, *yin* is the capacity for the configurative ordering to become **manifest** as realized plans. No building of anything takes place without order. The most frequently used understanding of *tohu* is chaos. However, even on a mundane, non-abstract physical basis, seeming chaos has order in it. Even a randomly tangled clump of yarn, knotted and hopelessly snarled has order in it or it couldn't exist as physical matter. Protons, neutrons, chemical bonds and electron shells exist due to the imposition of ordered organization. This imposed ordering of organization is no less in evidence in ideas and language.

Although the stand I am taking is that *tohu* provides the force of organization and the generating capacity for order and exactitude, it **itself** is unfathomable and has no internal observable order. In fact, *tohu* can also be understood and translated as "void" or "without form." On a meta-level, the nature of *tohu* itself is completely inscrutable and it is thoroughly outside of our understanding. The Ramban describes this when he refers to *tohu* and says that any name, once assigned to it, is instantly regretted and another name is sought. The word *tohu* is related to the word *tohei*, תוהא, regrets, and this is the Ramban's reference in this regard. This leaves me to say that *tohu* and the *hyule* of its kind are themselves void and without form. We can only identify *tohu*'s **influence**, and not itself.

By way of analogy, it would be as if the only apprehension we could have of anything that could come to our perception from our environment would be if it were to be illuminated by bright, full-spectrum light. Without that light, we are lost and confounded as to the distinctions of our surroundings, rendering them null and absent of identification. In essence, those same environmental markers cease to exist when the lights are off. The source of the light may still be present, but unless it illuminates something, we make no sense of it. Therefore, *tohu* is itself, as the usual translations say, chaos, void, and without form. But it does not impart chaos or wipe out existence or obliterate substance. Rather, it instigates order, enervates structure and design, and enables the manifestation of form.

We can now take a moment to recapitulate the convergence of definitions, and the congruence of the essence of the abstractions. We must recall, however, that there are different levels of those abstractions at work here and that, for example, earth on one level is not congruent completely with earth on another level. With that in mind, first there is *hyule*, of which there are two types. One is linked with heaven and *yang*, fire, light, and *tohu*. The other is linked with earth and *yin*, water, darkness, and, of course, with *bohu*. Employing physical terms, we can expand the examples of the complementary pairs of opposites to matter (*yin*) and energy (*yang*), inside (*yin*) and outside (*yang*), female (*yin*) and male (*yang*), cold (*yin*) and hot (*yang*), slow (*yin*) and fast (*yang*), space (*yin*) and time (*yang*), etc. The point here is that our physical world is displaying the ordering of everything by dual-natured forces. Further, this not only applies to the physical world, observable by us through our senses enabled through our nervous systems. It also applies to the abstract world of pure, Divine ideation, as it applies to our world, in which we share just a small portion through our own cognitive faculties. As it says in the *Siddur*, "[T]he precision of the cosmos is evident all over the earth to any observer."[25] However, none of that precision, driven by *tohu*, could be in evidence without the concretizing power of *bohu*.

Before I leave the discussion of *tohu*, we need to discuss the nature of

---

25   Ibid.

the *kav*, the *kav tohu*, which we have been investigating. Fundamentally, this is the *kav ohr ein sof*—the ray (line) of the light of *ein sof*. All of spiritual and physical Creation is constructed using this light. Isaac Luria, the Ari, describes the nature of this *kav*:

> He then drew a simple concentrated ray from the infinite light into the vacated space... The upper extremity of this ray touched the infinite light of ein sof that surrounded the space (the challal) and extended toward its center. It was through this ray, serving as a conduit, that the light of ein sof was brought down to spread into the entire vacated space.

The essential question about the *kav ohr Ein Sof* is, "What effects did the introduction of the light of the *Ein Sof* generate in the *challal*?" Without going through all of the details of what is understood of this process from *Kabbalah*, about which the *Etz Chaim*, the *Zohar*, and the *Bahir* speak, along with the many commentators on these works, I am going to suggest a basic framework. First, the original single point from which God's light was distanced to the sides of the conceptual space is the focal destination of the *kav ohr Ein Sof* as it is brought down and then spreads throughout the *challal*. This "speck" at the center of the space is considered the "place" (the actual point) from which the entire universe was founded and expanded. This is the primal singularity from which the universe manifested through the Big Bang and is also the point at which we find the Shettiah Stone (אבן שתיה or אבן שתייה), upon which the Holy of Holies of the ancient Temple in Jerusalem was located, according to the Ramban in his Torah commentary. In the *Zohar*, regarding this one point, it says: "Rabbi Chiya said to Rabbi Jose, the holy and mysterious One graved in a hidden recess one point. In that, He enclosed the whole of Creation, as one who locks up all his treasures in a palace, under one key, which is therefore as valuable as all that is stored up in that palace."[26]

Tohu confers order but is itself void and without form (i.e., chaos).

---

26   Sperling, *The Zohar*, p. 13.

The injection of the *kav ohr Ein Sof* into the *challal* is the introduction of order and precision (*kav tohu*) imposed on the void. This hearkens back to our detailed discussion of *Elokim* from chapter 3. However, for this order to be able to evidence itself, it must have a substratum that yields the potential for manifestation, through which the imposition of precision can bring about and evidence something, anything. In reference to the earth, in its primordial, archetypal rendition, the Ramban says, "Now, with this creation (the *hyule* of earth), which was like a small fine speck and had no substance, were created (in potential), all the creations in the heavens and on the earth." This last reference to heaven and earth is clearly indicating a stepped-down rendition of the archetypes of heaven and earth. These are the heaven and earth that have been made (*ya'as*—יעש) and formed (*yatzar*—יצר) from the interplay of the powers inhered in the two *hyule* of heaven and earth, and which themselves constitute the manifestations derived from the power imparted by the archetypal earth. This comprises everything that was made and formed from the two *hyule* that were created *ex nihilo*. That said, if we regard the *hyule* of earth as being allied to the speck, it is then easier to understand why the *Sefer Yetzirah* says, "He created substance from *tohu*, and made that which was nothing something." This does not mean that *tohu* changes into *bohu*. It means that with the "target" of *bohu* in the receiving role of the speck, *tohu* through the medium of the *kav ohr Ein Sof* causes to manifest and make nothing something.

At this point in our discussion, let us look at a perspective that relies on the nature of laser light and that can also be found within the writings of Lurianic *Kabbalah*. This is the nature of the built-in relationship between the light of the *kav ohr Ein Sof* and its minor cousin, the light that we can see. The *kav ohr Ein Sof* is the force imposing order and precision on what is otherwise undifferentiated potential for manifestation. It is analogous to and has properties akin to a beam of light from a laser. The wavelength of a beam of laser light is uniform and singular. Light in a laser beam itself is coherent and tracks a straight path. That is, it is different from the light of the sun, which can be broken up into the different wavelengths that produce the rainbow, or a light bulb whose light diffuses in all directions once it has been emitted. Laser light's trajectory does not diffuse, running straight and true for hundreds of thousands of miles in some cases, depending on the strength of the beam and the medium through which it runs.

Laser light has the capacity to carry information in the form of structured data, which can be transmitted in the form of ones and zeroes (on and off) encoded into the beam of light. The light that travels the fiber-optic cable superhighway of the Internet carries a corpuscular transmission of data (packets of "ons" and "offs," better known as the ones and zeroes of computer code). In his commentary on the Torah, Rabbi Elie Munk says, "It (the *kav ohr Ein Sof*) is composed of an infinity of isolated points and pours forth in an 'atomized,' corpuscular form. This world of punctiform lights, *olam ha'nekudos*...[is]...involved in the organization of matter..." He describes it as a matter-building force and refers to the Ari giving it a correspondence with *tohu*.

The information in the laser-generated light traveling in a fiber optic cable, with the order and structure encoded in it, can only be displayed and observed when it is received at a destination capable of decoding the data. Even if we could look directly into the beam of the laser light running in the fiber optic cable—which we cannot, due to the severe retinal damage that would result—we cannot decode the information in it. It has no meaning without the correlated means of decoding it.

Albeit by analogy, this is the same as the dynamic of the interplay of *tohu* and *bohu*. *Tohu* imposes order and structure, while conveying information, and *bohu* is there to receive it, decode it, manifest the instruction, and make nothing something. As well, the light of the *kav ohr Ein Sof* is much like the light of the Torah, with its corpuscular transmission of order and design in the form of the letters, their inherent number values, the words, and the spaces between the letters and words. The Architect of the universe "looked" into the Torah in order to create the world, transmitting His intention through its structure.

ובהו

The word "substance" is used by the Ramban and Rabbeinu ben Asher in their discussions while referring to the term *hyule*. However, if one loses track of the proper context when referring to the word "substance," it can certainly distort the actual intent for which it is being used. We have to clarify which definition of substance we are going to carry forward from here and in which context. Both of the *hyule*, that of *shamayim* and that of *aretz*, are referred to as substances by our Sages. As mentioned earlier, this use is really a misnomer, as what is really meant is that these are substance-less substances. After all, this is an abstraction, unlike substances that are made in the physical world. Use of the word "substance" when referring to *hyule* is merely a convenient linguistic reference. This is in lieu of some actually accurate descriptor. Of course, to coin a completely accurate word for *hyule* in Hebrew is to run into the problem that the Ramban describes when referring to *tohu* when he says that any name, once assigned, is instantly regretted and another name is sought. In any case, the word "substance" used in the context of describing *hyule*, is a word that does not mean anything physical at all, even though that is to where the mind tends to run immediately.

As it has in other paired abstractions we have analyzed, here the *vav* holds a critical role in the understanding of *bohu*. It has us read *tohu va'vohu* together, in one single construction, linking them together back to *ha'aretz*, in order to clarify its inner nature. Therefore, it behooves us to treat it that way and bear in mind that we cannot understand *bohu* without its relationship with *tohu*. The Ramban asks, "[A]nd what is *bohu*? Something that has substance, as if it were written *bo hu* (בו הוא)—It is in it." What does that mean: "It is in it"? What does the first "it" mean? The second "it," obviously, is referring to *bohu* itself. However, we must bear in mind that this *bohu* is not, itself, physical in any way.

Rabbeinu Bachya ben Asher and the *Zohar*, among other sources, point us in the following direction. They say that the entire universe grew from a miniscule speck (the original singularity). At least by inference, this speck is composed of some substance. The position and the language I am taking on is that the quality of this substance is that of a concretizing, centripetal nature. In fact, it is the repository of all and everything that is to come into physical existence. This is *bohu* ordered by *tohu*, leading to the appearance of the primordial black hole, out of which came all matter and energy together—the resultant from the Big Bang.

As to the first "it" in "It is in it," this is of the same nature and quality as the *hyule* of earth. This is the centripetal, concretizing, condensing force in the universe. This is the prototypical, archetypal *yin*. However, it too, like *tohu* without *bohu*, is void without *tohu*. In the absence of the force of organization and order and precision, it is null, empty of all form. Once fertilized by *tohu*, *bohu* harbors all things possible in the world. This is the potential cornucopia of the diversity of everything/ no-thing. It is the root of all manifestation in the physical universe.

תהו ובהו

The *vav*, about which we have written extensively before, declares the inseparability of *tohu* and *bohu*. We could say, "And the earth was (inherently) lines of organizational force and stones of potentiation for concretization." We could also use the terms *tzurah* and *chomer* (צורה וחומר) which are generally understood to mean "form" and "substance" in the abstract. Form (צורה) is obviously the organizational force and substance (חומר) is the potential for manifestation. In the wilderness of Sinai, Betzalel was chosen to build the tabernacle, the *Mishkan*. In a citation from the Gemara in *Berachot*, "Betzalel [בצלאל, which means in the shadow (image—בצל) of God (אל)] knew how to combine the letters by which the heavens and earth were created."[27] According to the Ramban, Betzalel's understanding of the structure of creation enabled him to make the architecture of the Tabernacle correspond to the architecture of the universe.

This takes us right back to the speculation outlined above, that the *kav ohr Ein Sof* is the ray of the encoded force for organizing *bohu* at the very center of the *challal*, and that the corpuscular nature of the encoded letters, words, and spaces of the Torah (which itself is frequently referred to as being light) can be understandable to us using the analogy of laser light and fiber optic cable. *Tohu* gives us strict instructional

---

27   Israel Schneider, *The Gemara: Tractate Berachos* (Brooklyn: Mesorah, 1997) vol. II, chap. 9, p. 55a³, fn. 40.

order, the perfect tool for the Master Architect of the universe. *Bohu* is the potential for **all manifestation** that is permitted by the ordering inherent in the information from the *kav ohr Ein Sof*. This is everything possible in the universe that God willed into existence. The *Zohar* says that *Elokim* "graved" the letters inside the *challal*. Given that the letters are also numbers, the Hebrew alphabet is the data potential for all manifestations of reality that God willed through the letters, numbers, and spaces combined. Again, by analogy, this is like the ultimate encryption algorithm. Clearly, the Fibonacci sequence, Pi (π), Phi (ϕ), geometry, and all other mathematical and spatial relationships and arrangements are found within the ordered information imposed by the supreme Architect.

CHAPTER SIX

YOM ECHAD: SECOND VERSE, SECOND CONCEIT

בְּרֵא שִׁית (בְּרֵאשִׁית) בְּרָא אֱלֹקִים אֵת הַשָּׁמַיִם וְאֵת הָאָרֶץ. וְהָאָרֶץ הָיְתָה תֹהוּ וָבֹהוּ וְחֹשֶׁךְ עַל פְּנֵי תְהוֹם וְרוּחַ אֱלֹקִים מְרַחֶפֶת עַל פְּנֵי הַמָּיִם. וַיֹּאמֶר אֱלֹקִים יְהִי אוֹר וַיְהִי אוֹר. וַיַּרְא אֱלֹקִים אֶת הָאוֹר כִּי טוֹב וַיַּבְדֵּל אֱלֹקִים בֵּין הָאוֹר וּבֵין הַחֹשֶׁךְ. וַיִּקְרָא אֱלֹקִים לָאוֹר יוֹם וְלַחֹשֶׁךְ קָרָא לָיְלָה וַיְהִי עֶרֶב וַיְהִי בֹקֶר יוֹם אֶחָד.

SECOND CONCEIT

וְחֹשֶׁךְ עַל פְּנֵי תְהוֹם.

A more common translation of this phrase is, "With darkness on the surface of the deep." Of note, here, is the phrase *al p'nei* (עַל פְּנֵי) [*tehom*] as mentioned above. Due to the proximity of these words and their likeness to exactly the same construction only half a verse away, in *al p'nei* (עַל פְּנֵי) [*ha'mayim*], this phrase cannot be understood by itself alone. The context I am going to use is the link between the two phrases in this second verse.

This phrase can be best understood once we question all three segments of it in order to establish definitional clarity. It is not enough to believe that we understand what these words mean without establishing the context for their appearance. First, let us place ourselves in the narrative. Here we are in the details of the manifesting Creation. There is no thing other than the speck that exists. From an astrophysics perspective, we are only at the advent of the singularity, we have not gotten to the big bang itself yet. Time does not exist yet, nor does space. This means that the *choshech* is not what we conceive of as the darkness born of the absence of light. It calls into question what we understand about the nature of the deep and why the surface of it and the surface of the water are related. We must also bear in mind that *tehom* and *mayim* are also archetypes and, as such, we must understand them on that level.

וחשך

In *Kabbalah*, this darkness is described as a palpable darkness. Given that there is absolutely nothing other than the initial speck of the original singularity at this point in the account of Creation, this has to be something incredibly dense. If we recall the description from chapter 2, whereby God constricted His light to the sides of a conceptual space, we then have the resulting darkness of the *challal*. On first examination, this darkness appears to have been derived from the withdrawal of God's light alone, therefore, seeming as if it is produced from something previously existing. However, the *challal* results from a creation *ex nihilo*: the *tzimtzum* and the related *challal* were a creation out of absolute nihility. About this, Scripture states in Isaiah 45:7 that God forms (יוצר, from previously existing material) light and creates (ובורא, from the verb *bara*, creation *ex nihilo*—ברא) darkness: "*Yotzer ohr u'vorei choshech.*" Aryeh Kaplan writes, "Darkness is a completely novel concept and has no relationship to God. It is therefore 'created'—'something from nothing.'"[28] Rabbi Kaplan cites the *Guide for the Perplexed* and the *Bahir* as his sources for this perspective.

This is the primeval darkness of all of Creation. It is incumbent on us to recall the hierarchy of the terms as they are introduced in the Torah in their archetypal and then stepped-down versions, being mindful of the distinctions brought about through context and placement in the

---

28   Kaplan, *Innerspace*, 26.

text. This is leading up to the introduction of light in the next verse. We must bear in mind that the light that God withdrew to the sides of the conceptual space is the light of the *Ein Sof*, not the light we encounter on a daily basis nor what we encounter in the next verse. The light in the next verse is the light that flooded the universe along with the physical expansion of the universe.

This *choshech*, an entirely "thickened" creation, is the virtual opposite of the totally spiritual nature of God's light. The light of the *Ein Sof* is the epitome of the ethereal, at the far end (*yang*) of the *yin/yang* spectrum, and this created darkness (*yin*) is at the other end. The darkness of the *challal* could be described as the ultimate density, at the far other end of the scale, virtually purely *yin*. As a brief refresher, *yin* is concretizing and centripetal, dense and sinks to the center. And *yang* is its opposite. If we search the manifest world for the most fitting reflection of what this could possibly mean, we are forced to recognize one option: a black hole. The physicists of modern times concur with the Ramban and Rabbeinu Bachya ben Asher in the notion that the universe was founded from a single small speck. They say that the entire universe grew from this iota, this miniscule concentration of potentiality for manifestation. By reason, this speck is composed of some substance. This is the original singularity, the initial, solitary, nearly infinitely small and dense black hole, out of which the entire universe emerged in one inconceivable explosion of seething intensity of transforming electromagnetic energy (light) and matter. Here we revisit the understanding from our discussion of *bohu*. That is, *bo hu* (בו הוא)—"It is in it." What is in it? The entire universe: all matter (including dark matter) and energy (including dark energy) that exists today!

These similarities found between the modern scientific description of the earliest portions of Creation and the ancient mystical view of the *Briah* from Torah are striking. When they are in concordance, it's easy to say how validating each is to the other. However, we should recoil at the urge to validate Torah with science. For that matter, it's problematic to adopt a "see, I told you so" attitude of superiority over the fact that Torah "knew" of these truths about creation many centuries before science could reach them.

How should we grapple with the dilemma of science and Torah disagreeing, as they certainly do, over the age of the universe, being orders of magnitude different from each other? In the end, comparing the timelines in Torah or science in relation to Creation is specious if it is for the sake of claiming the rights to declaring "right" or "wrong." Arguably, both are right. This is because context is everything. There is no difficulty adhering to the established ideas within each understanding, whether the world of Torah or the world of science. To cross the borders can create conflict, confusion, and discord. Keeping an open heart and mind as to the difference in approaches for understanding our world is paramount for an enlightened mind.

The current scientific, astrophysical understanding of the beginning of the universe follows extremely closely to the unfolding of the *Briah* from the perspective of the Torah, particularly the kabbalistic view. Given the historical changeability of scientific theories, to emphasize the correctness of the scientific view over the Torah would be misguided. The Torah perspective, however, because of its Divine root, is foundational, because of its timeless transcendence.

על פני

Returning to the text, there are two basic choices of how to render this composite expression, "on the face of," or "on the surface of." Although the net result is essentially the same, we are going to employ "on the surface of" for the most part, because it is the surface of something that is going to be the focus of our attention for the remainder of this verse.

תהום

The conventional understanding of this word is "the deep." Questions spring to mind from this. Deep implies shallow, so what is the relativity that is being described here—given that it is **the** deep, what is the implication? What exactly is it that is deep? How deep is deep, really? Is this a metaphor or a description of something that one could conceive of being measured, relating to the march toward the physical manifestation of the universe, with its inherent amenability to being measured?

The deep is clearly an archetype in the account of Creation. As it is, **the** deep, it transcends comparisons, rendering it unique and not definable by contrast. As such, we have reached a predecessor state prior to the advent of the light in the third verse. It is dark through and through and on its surface. This is the *challal*—a unique creation of darkness as archetype. We are then led to inexorably refer to this as the original singularity just preceding the beginning of the expansion into our physical universe: the original black hole prior to the Big Bang. Physicists describe the strength of the gravitational field of any black hole as being infinite, or at least approaching infinity. By virtue of that enormous gravity, not even light can escape from its surface. This renders it completely dark to any outside observer. In fact, the nature of any black hole is that it is detectable because of its gravitational influence on other bodies, not by observation of it itself. The characteristics and motions of other bodies and gases in proximity to currently observable black holes in the universe are determined by the nature of the black hole's prodigious gravitational force.

In the case of the original singularity, colloquially, the mother of all black holes, the status of its properties can be described in the following way: Mathematically speaking, gravitation tends to infinity, as density tends to infinity, as size tends to the infinitely small, and as the Big Bang initially begins, temperatures tend to the infinitely high. The depth of the deep is infinite as well. It is the speck referred to by the Ramban and Rabbeinu Bachya ben Asher, and as such it has the primeval property of *bo hu*. It is certainly coherent to equate the *challal* and its properties with the deep. Both are a created darkness and both satisfy the necessary and sufficient conditions for Creation to advance to materialization from the abstract. The *Zohar* refers to the darkness of Creation as a lamp of darkness. This could mean that it radiates darkness, or that its nature generates darkness around itself. This, too, fits the description of the *challal* as the original singularity (the original primal black hole) and as the deep, and it being inhered with the meaning of *bo hu*. For **everything** is in it!

CHAPTER SEVEN

YOM ECHAD: SECOND VERSE, THIRD CONCEIT

ברא שית (בראשית) ברא אלקים את השמים ואת הארץ. והארץ
היתה תהו ובהו וחשך על פני תהום ורוח אלקים מרחפת על פני
המים. ויאמר אלקים יהי אור ויהי אור. וירא אלקים את האור
כי טוב ויבדל אלקים בין האור ובין החשך. ויקרא אלקים לאור
יום ולחשך קרא לילה ויהי ערב ויהי בקר יום אחד.

THIRD CONCEIT

ורוח אלקים מרחפת על פני המים.

This is the finalizing sub-phrase in the second verse. *V'ruach Elokim merachephet al p'nei ha'mayim.* This is the first instance of *Elokim* interacting with His Creation. This is, until this point in the narrative, unprecedented. This is no longer merely a statement of state that is being narrated. The first verse mentions *Elokim* only once. That mention is made within the context of the attribute of God that is responsible for the unfolding of the manifestations of contrast: that is, duality. All of the first verse is taking place in the realm of Creation being brought into existence *ex nihilo* (ברא).

As a new distinction in the narrative of the account of Creation, the two words *ruach Elokim* taken together signify one single ideational emblem. God employs it to implement the forces of Creation acting on the original singularity. In order for such an interaction as is being described to have a new meaning, the inherent nature of *Elokim* as perfect architect of the precise drawing of distinctions, is being employed for bringing a new distinction into existence. This is the essential prerequisite in the advent of the making of light in the next verse. The nature of the second half of this sub-phrase is that it is declaring that movement and change are the generators of what is coming. No longer is it creation *ex nihilo* or a characterization of it that is being narrated. Something is happening to and within that which is already created, the speck, resulting in it being fashioned into the opening of the actual materialization of Creation. What has been in the ideational realm of God's archetypal cognitive emblems now transforms into the forces acting on the raw materials of the universe aborning. We say in the morning's prayer liturgy from Isaiah 45:7, "*Yotzer ohr, u'vorei choshech*—He forms light and creates darkness."

ורוח אלקים

The word *ruach* (רוח) can mean wind or breath or spirit. In the context of the Creation narrative, it can only mean "spirit." As it is tied to *Elokim*, as we discussed at great length earlier, it tells us that this attribute is the source of the action in this conceit of the second verse. This interpretation comes alive when viewed in relation to the 147th psalm, where it says, "ישב רוחו ילזו מים—He blows his wind and the waters flow." Clearly, there is no wind, as no air or luminaries or planets exist as yet in the narrative of Creation. Therefore, the most fitting sense will have to be either breath or spirit. While through an anthropomorphism it could be breath, this, too, is contextually wrong for the passage. So, it could only be spirit, and the nature of the spirit of God is that it inheres with movement. This is hinted at in relation to the alternative translation for this word, wind, as wind **is** specifically movement.

Given this perspective, I can now recontextualize the understanding and translation of this verse from Psalms and relate it directly to the second half of the second verse of the first *yom*. Here are some possibilities:

- "He moves His spirit and the water(s) flow."
- "He rests His spirit on the water(s) and they flow."

- "He hovers His spirit on the water(s) and they flow."
- "His spirit (*Elokim*'s) moves and the water(s) flow."

If we take all four of these alternatives and allow them to suffuse into each other, we come away with a sense that, put into narrative form, would go something like this. The *ruach Elokim* has the nature of movement that generates order and produces new distinctions on what has already been created *ex nihilo*. This is evidenced from the lengthy earlier discussions on the nature of the attribute of *Elokim* from chapter 3.

The *ruach Elokim* acting on the surface of the water(s) generates a stunning state change, and with its advent, movement and ordering begin to accelerate and manifest. This is the required and fitting force for the first micro-micro seconds after the Big Bang. It generates the unique transformation that results in the "explosion" of the Big Bang. This itself generates the roiling sea of subatomic particles that wink in and out of existence, which are intermixed with pure energy (electromagnetic radiation). This mixture of matter and energy, labeled as "plasma," is the immediate predecessor condition for the bursting forth of light when God says, "Let there be light." No source of power except the Power Above All Powers could possibly generate what was necessary to have **anything**, including light, emerge from the virtually infinite gravity of the singularity. Only God could (can) do this.

מרחפת

It is the spirit of *Elokim* that is hovering over the surface of the water(s). This is likened to a mother bird flapping her wings over her nest, in which the fledgling baby birds are clamoring for food from her. She doesn't actually land on the nest, maintaining her position separately. However, she also feeds her chicks by touching her beak inside theirs, as she disgorges the food she's brought for them.

This word is a present tense rendering. The beginning of this verse is written in the past tense. However, as discussed extensively in that phrase (והארץ היתה תהו ובהו) in chapter 5, the tense of the construction is not compatible with the sense of the progression of the narrative. Hence, the relevance of the citation given earlier,[29] where it says, "[W]hereas the first half of the verse speaks in the past tense [*haytah*—היתה], this phrase [*merachephet al ha'mayim*—מרחפת על פני המים] uses the present tense."

This hovering is a reflection, I believe, of the phrase describing the onset of Creation from the *Zohar*, "touching and yet not touching." This is indicative of the relationship of God with His Creation, in which He is in it and not in it, simultaneously. This notion is also reminiscent of the discussion from chapter 1. The ultimate paradox of God's presence and absence from the world is inferred from this phrasing. There is the influence upon, but not inclusion within, the utter state change that is taking place.

The flapping wings of the hovering mother bird stir the delicate feathers of her chicks and animate their response to her presence. The *ruach Elokim* stirs the surface of the deep and generates the "appearance" of the "water" that results (to be explained). As the singularity explodes due to the interaction of the *ruach Elokim* with it, the resultant is the amorphous sea of seething superheated subatomic particles and electromagnetic energy that is the Big Bang. As the particles wink in and out of existence, transforming from matter to energy and back again in mere fractions of fractions of fractions of a second, the expansion accelerates to inconceivable speeds and keeps expanding from there to this very day. As the expansion advances from the Big Bang itself, the heat of the newborn universe begins to fall from its highest temperature of more than 10^{32} degrees Kelvin.

על פני

As it was earlier in this verse in the case of *al p'nei*, על פני (*tehom*), on the surface of (the deep), we're choosing the phrase *al p'nei*, על פני (*ha'mayim*), to mean on the surface of (the water(s)). With the proximity of these words and their likeness to exactly the same construction only half a verse earlier, the analysis here should round out the earlier discussion and show further how they are linked. At this point in the narrative, we are exposing the details made available from the text that

---

relate to the interaction of the non-physical forces that generate the manifestation of Creation. There is no distinct thing that exists yet, as all is in the tremendous flux of pre-matter and undifferentiated energy. From an astrophysics perspective, we are now witnessing the expansion immediately following the Big Bang.

המים

At this point in the narrative, we need to address some questions that naturally arise from this word. We need to determine which water(s) we are talking about. First, from whence did this water come? It seems to have sprung into the narrative with no predecessor introduction. In addition, to what level of the manifestation of Creation has the narrative now progressed?

The word *mayim*, water, appeared in the first portion of the first verse bound up with *aish*, fire, in the word *shamayim*. The *Bahir* states that God "kneaded together fire and water to make *shamayim*." These ideas were presented at great length in chapter 3. In it we found the archetype of water as a crafting emblem of Creation. Here we find it again, except at this point it is more manifest and no longer archetypal. Nevertheless, the water here has its roots in the water as the archetypal ideational emblem from the first verse. Furthermore, since fire and water are bound up together to make heaven, as described in the first verse, it reveals water itself as the perfect resultant of *ruach Elokim* acting upon the surface of the *tehom*.

Since the turn of the twenty-first century, experimentation has been carried out to define the properties of the previously theorized plasma that resulted from the Big Bang. This plasma (the admixture of subatomic particles and energy inter-transforming into each other in ultra-rapid fashion immediately following the Big Bang) is referred to as the quark-gluon plasma. It is the manifestation of the matter/energy conversion predicted by Einstein's famous equations, such as $E = mc^2$. It was widely believed that this quark-gluon plasma—also described as a state of matter/energy where quarks and the strong force-carrying gluons have yet to condense into separate families of sub-atomic particles—would behave as a gas. However, in the early 2000s, culminating around 2010, physicists found that the quark-gluon plasma actually behaved like a "near-perfect liquid." What this means is that this "liquid" is virtually without any viscosity, essentially permitting free, frictionless flow. This conclusion has now been verified by experimentation and the characteristics have been determined to be those of a high-energy, high-temperature, intra-transforming, rapidly expanding "soup" of subatomic particles and virtually undifferentiated energy. This is the plasma as water.

All of the matter and all of the (electromagnetic) energy that ever was, is, and will be in the entire universe was unleashed from the primeval speck of a black hole in the form of this plasma. As visible light is one portion of the electromagnetic spectrum; it is a reasonable convention to say that all electromagnetic radiation is also legitimately nameable as light. During this phase, matter and energy were indistinctly confounded with each other. The intrinsic mass of this plasma was virtually nil, as matter and energy had not yet become distinct nor stably separate. Since the four fundamental forces of nature had not yet become distinct either, no separation of matter and energy had taken place. Those forces are gravity, the strong and weak nuclear forces, and electromagnetism. This was the state of manifestation that has come to be called by the name quark-gluon plasma.

This fluid of a virtually infinitely high temperature, estimated to have been dramatically higher than 10^{32} Kelvin (zero degrees Kelvin is called absolute zero, approximately 459.67 degrees below zero Fahrenheit), having the properties of a near-perfect liquid as the Ramban characterized so many centuries ago, clearly points us back toward the kneading together of *mayim* and *aish* to make *shamayim*, as described in the *Bahir*. This is the beginning of the unfolding of everything in the heavens coming into the realm of a manifest world. The archetype of *shamayim*, heaven, generates its imprint in the beginning of the physical universe. It manifests here, at the outset, in the formless, virtually massless, virtually infinitely hot, virtually perfect liquid that comprises the ultra-rapid expansion of the universe from the onset of the Big Bang. This manifestation of the tangible and measurable, even though in its own infancy, is the advent of the actualization of the archetype of *aretz*, earth.

CHAPTER EIGHT

YOM ECHAD: THIRD VERSE

בְּרֵא שִׁית (בראשית) בְּרֵא אלקים אֶת הַשָּׁמִים וְאֶת הָאָרֶץ. וְהָאָרֶץ הָיְתָה תֹּהוּ וָבֹהוּ וְחֹשֶׁךְ עַל פְּנֵי תְהוֹם וְרוּחַ אלקים מְרַחֶפֶת עַל פְּנֵי הַמִּים. וַיֹּאמֶר אלקים יְהִי אוֹר וַיְהִי אוֹר. וַיַּרְא אלקים אֶת הָאוֹר כִּי טוֹב וַיַּבְדֵּל אלקים בֵּין הָאוֹר וּבֵין הַחֹשֶׁךְ. וַיִּקְרָא אלקים לָאוֹר יוֹם וְלַחֹשֶׁךְ קָרָא לָיְלָה וַיְהִי עֶרֶב וַיְהִי בֹּקֶר יוֹם אֶחָד.

THIRD VERSE

וַיֹּאמֶר אלקים יְהִי אוֹר וַיְהִי אוֹר.

God said, "Let there be light and there was light."

It is widely agreed upon that this sentence and others like this declarative of God's "words," are statements depicting the enactment of the will of God. Obviously, God is not speaking in any kind of way that we could describe in anthropomorphic terms. Nor is God "saying" or cognizing something which we can actually, in truth, be capable of comprehending. Nevertheless, our Sages seem to agree that this is descriptive of the operations of (the "mind" of) God. When all of the words in the Torah are first introduced, they are ideational emblems. We remember that they are archetypes of some conceptual "reality" that can or could come to fruition in the material world that is our own. As such, given that it is *Elokim* that utters this, it must be a carving out of a feature of Creation from the background of all possible distinctions. This was discussed at length in chapter 3. However, given the stage of Creation in which this utterance is taking place, it is placed here in the narrative directly relating to the spectacular materialization of His created world resulting from the Big Bang.

ויאמר אלקים

This is the very first time that the ideational realm of God's creating is made explicit by His "giving voice" to a designation that establishes a new distinction. God has altered His relationship with His Creation. Before now, it is as if His "actions" are being narrated by some neutral third party: the three being *Elokim*, Creation itself, and the narrator. This change is going to generate an enormously important transformation in the impending destination of Creation from here onward. Although not explicitly referenced this way in the text, *Elokim* is now in the act of making or fashioning (*yotzar*, יצר and *ya'as*, יעש), not creating (like the verb *bara* of the first verse would indicate). Thus, this is producing a change of state in what is already created. Here is a distinction of immense significance. In a very real sense, Creation, specifically, is over. Along the path of the narrative so far, that which God created *ex nihilo* has already been created. Creation is now being made and fashioned and evolved into the world of existence in time and space.

However, all that being said, it's important to remind ourselves that the frame of the apparent sequential events, stages, or states that are indicated by the linearity of the text itself really belies the true nature of Creation. It is fully logical that the singularity had to precede the Big Bang. On the level of the understanding imparted by physics, the plasma had to appear only after the initiation of the expansion from the original singularity. In the Torah's terms, these seemingly distinct states are not so clearly distinguishable as being sequential in time. They are taking place in a "conceptual or logical time dimension," to quote Aryeh Kaplan again.

While the overlay of the science of physics on top of the Torah's text has the flavor of a perfect fit, we have to acknowledge that it is a virtual impossibility that our understanding can produce a full congruence, nor, perhaps, should it. After all, the Torah is, by its very nature, inscrutable in a spiritual dimension, while the physics of creation is inscrutable in the realm of the equations that make it up, for those of us who simply can't grasp the intricacies of the math. While the two varieties of impenetrability are like each other, they are not the same. Torah is eternal and immutable and the understanding from science is subject to the statement "on further review..." In the end, we can only marvel at the fact that in the last hundred years we are beginning to glimpse what appear to be stunning congruences of understanding and scope between Torah and science.

יהי אור ויהי אור

"Let there be light and there was light." *Ruach Elokim* has already touched and not touched (read: induced, without being changed itself, like the nature of a catalyst, without which things do not change, but is itself unchanged in the process) the surface of the water (read: that which has the properties of a formless, massless, infinitely hot, near-perfect liquid that comprises the soup of subatomic particles and light [electromagnetic radiation] released in the very first instants after the Big Bang) from the Deep (read: the original singularity from which the entire sum of matter and energy in the entire universe sprang almost fourteen billion years ago). Something is about to happen now that is of an utterly different nature. The intermixture of energy and matter in the existing indistinct state is a roiling fluid in which the forces of gravity, the strong and weak nuclear forces and electromagnetism have not yet become separated.

With the utterance, "Let there be light," the change of state required to have photons uncouple from matter takes place. Micro-micro-micro seconds before God's utterance, within the conditions of the plasma, free photons (essentially bundles of electromagnetic energy) are colliding with and inter-transforming with subatomic particles. Photons would then not be in evidence to an "outside observer," (obviously not actually physically possible nor conceivable) and they cannot shine independently, because they are being trapped by the subatomic particles of the post-Big Bang primordium. Should it have been possible to observe this state it would have been completely dark, since no light could escape the matter-energy mixture. A micro-brief moment of time earlier, the rate of expansion of the primeval fireball from the Big Bang suddenly exceeded the speed of light. This is the one-time occurrence known as the Inflationary Period. Along with this expansion, the ultra-hot temperature is falling.

The time citations of hundreds of thousands, or millions, or billions of years represented here and elsewhere in this writing are conventions adopted from current scientific understandings of how the universe unfolded. They should not be construed to be contradictory to or refutations of the spans of years in scriptural texts that relate to *Ma'aseh Bereishit*. Time references from one context to the other do not apply, as discussed near the end of chapter 6. So, from current perspectives in the physical sciences, during about the next 700,000 years, the temperature of the expanding universe continued to fall and eventually reached about 3000 degrees Kelvin. Reckoning this by human clock time until today, only five thousandths of a percent of the age of the universe had passed at this stage. Slightly beyond that time, photons uncoupled from matter. The much cooler, expanded universe released those photons, resulting in an inconceivable paroxysm of light that filled the entire universe. This light had no source like the sun or another star. In Hebrew, this is *ohr* (אור), but it has no physical source from which it emanates (מ'אור), like the sun or stars. This *ohr* (אור) is the primordial light to which this verse in the Torah refers. The remnants of this light comprise the so-called cosmic microwave background radiation, whose temperature is currently measured at approximately 3.4 degrees Kelvin, and which was first discovered in 1964. It is this remaining light (remembering that light is a form of electromagnetic energy [energy = electromagnetic radiation = light]) that has been taken to be the scientific proof of the Big Bang.

This was partially validated (March 2014) by the analysis of findings from observations that evidence the so-called gravitational waves first proposed by Einstein in 1916 in his general theory of relativity. In 1980, physicist Alan Guth formally proposed that instead of the universe beginning as a rapidly and evenly expanding fireball, it suddenly inflated in size extremely rapidly from a tiny piece of already minutely expanded space. It then became exponentially larger in a fraction of a second.

However, as Guth, professor of physics at MIT, immediately realized, certain predictions in his scenario contradicted the observed data. In the early 1980s, Russian physicist Andrei Linde modified the model into a concept called "new inflation" and again to "eternal chaotic inflation," both of which generated predictions that closely matched actual observations of the sky. Then, in March of 2014, the presence of gravitational waves, first predicted by Einstein and then also by Linde, a professor of physics at Stanford, were confirmed. They were detected in the signals of the cosmic microwave background radiation. Linde could not hide his excitement about the news, when he said, "These results are a smoking gun for inflation, because alternative theories do not predict such a signal. This is something I had been hoping to see for thirty years."

The March 2014 detection of gravitational waves and the consequent implications, were confirmed and validated by the gravitational waves that were detected on September 14, 2015, by both of the twin **L**aser **I**nterferometer **G**ravitational-Wave **O**bservatory (LIGO) detectors, located in Livingston, Louisiana, and Hanford, Washington, in the United States. The incident that produced these waves occurred when two black holes suddenly merged approximately 1.3 billion years ago. These results taken together produce the definitive finding for the accuracy of the so-called Standard Model, including the notion of cosmic inflation.

The light of the expanding and cooling universe matches the light of this verse. How amazing that this expression of current science is in so much agreement with the commentaries of the Ramban and Rabbeinu Bachya ben Asher. This state of the light is a distinct and immensely important marker in the genesis of creation through Torah and nature.

CHAPTER NINE

YOM ECHAD: FOURTH VERSE, FIRST CONCEIT

ברא שית (בראשית) ברא אלקים את השמים ואת הארץ. והארץ היתה תהו ובהו וחשך על פני תהום ורוח אלקים מרחפת על פני המים. ויאמר אלקים יהי אור ויהי אור. וירא אלקים את האור כי טוב ויבדל אלקים בין האור ובין החשך. ויקרא אלקים לאור יום ולחשך קרא לילה ויהי ערב ויהי בקר יום אחד.

FIRST CONCEIT

וירא אלקים את האור כי טוב.
And God saw that the light was good.

This is no ordinary seeing, even for God. While this could be a handy anthropomorphism, it is clearly disclosing something to us about the relationship that God has with this manifestation of Creation. This statement is not here to tell us that God "took a look" at what He had fashioned and after noting its nature, realized for the first time that it was good.

I believe it is fitting to interpret this verse with the following idea in mind: This is one step in a progression. As such, "good" can only mean that the light was fitting and suitable for the actualization of the purposes for which Creation was brought about. This is not a statement of contrast with bad, or judgment on a moral or value scale. It is simply a declaration that God's creation is (so far at this point in the narrative) perfectly suited to fulfill its purpose and will remain in existence for the life of the created world. This is the way the Artscroll *Ramban* commentary renders this idea: "And the establishment of the permanent existence of those things is called 'seeing that it is good.'"[30] It is well to remember at this point that from *Kabbalah* we know that God created His world in order to bestow His ultimate good on His creation. Could it really be otherwise that the light would be anything but good, and, therefore, perfectly suitable and fitting for His purpose? In addition, the light that God "sees" as being good is still here. It has existed since the cosmic fireball from the Big Bang cooled enough approximately 14 billion years ago to release the photons. Once again, time citations like this one, on the order of billions of years, are conventions adopted from the current scientific thinking that dates the physical universe. They should not be construed to be contradictory to or refutations of the spans of years in scriptural texts that relate to *Ma'aseh Bereishit*. This light exists in the form of the cosmic microwave background radiation that Penzias and Wilson discovered in 1964.

The second portion of this verse's description of the separation of light and darkness has mostly been interpreted to mean that darkness is bad, since good and bad are the usual companions of contrast on a certain scale. I believe that the evidence will show unequivocally that the separation of light and darkness as well as the other separations enumerated in the narrative of Creation are utterly necessary and therefore, very good for God's purpose for the created world.

---

30 Yaakov Blinder, *Ramban: The Torah with Ramban's Commentary*, vol. 1 (Brooklyn: Mesorah, 2004), p. 33.

CHAPTER TEN

YOM ECHAD: FOURTH VERSE, SECOND CONCEIT

ברא שית (בראשית) ברא אלקים את השמים ואת הארץ. והארץ
היתה תהו ובהו וחשך על פני תהום ורוח אלקים מרחפת על פני
המים. ויאמר אלקים יהי אור ויהי אור. וירא אלקים את האור
כי טוב ויבדל אלקים בין האור ובין החשך. ויקרא אלקים לאור
יום ולחשך קרא לילה ויהי ערב ויהי בקר יום אחד.

SECOND CONCEIT

ויבדל אלקים בין האור ובין החשך.
And God separated between the light and (between) the
darkness.

We return once again to the nature of the attribute of *Elokim*. We're looking further into the attribute of *Elokim* from the perspective of its most abstract nature as a Divine power. It is this power which is the pure, perfect architect of exactitude. It is the power above all powers of pure and perfect judgment, distinguishing "this" from "not-this," rigorously exact and precise in His "actions." Being the attribute that is the generator of contrast in our universe, it is the necessary and sufficient requirement for the creation of duality.

This separating of light from darkness has been commented on, written about, and discussed for millennia. The result from the familiar commentaries is that darkness is labeled as bad, and the idea that darkness is inherently evil and bad is confirmed. However, referencing back to the discussion about evil in chapter 2, the archetypal evil is not bad, it is a necessary creation for the sake of a world in which human beings have free will. For a universe built for two, this separation is an essential state of affairs and one perfectly granted by the inherent nature of *Elokim*. Light and darkness must co-exist, being mutually interdependent and contrasting each with the other, but only once they are past the state of their being intermixed with each other. Were the light and darkness not to be separated, we would never have gotten to the point where matter and energy were distinct. While I respect and accept the interpretation that after this light dawned, it was put aside for the righteous in the next world, for our purposes I am not making references in the realm of the theological. The domain of our concern is narrowly confined to the cosmological. Therefore, the theological realm is not within our purview and will not be a concern for our purposes. This darkness, it must be added, is not the same as the darkness of the *challal*, which was a created, palpable darkness.

It is reasonable, albeit speculative, to suggest that this darkness is matter and the light is energy. Having emerged from each other's grasp from within the plasma after the Big Bang, it appears more reasonable that there is an interdependent relationship between them according to Einstein's famous equation, $E = mc^2$. Yet, separate they must be for the sake of Creation's advancement toward a perfect state for the existence of conscious life.

This phrase establishes that the light released from the primordial plasma will not go back to being intermingled with superheated quarks ever again. With the sudden appearance of brilliant light (אור) permeating the entire expanding, manifesting universe, the era of the super-heated plasma is over, and the decoupling of photons from matter is accomplished. It was so effective, in fact, that once photons uncoupled from matter after the Big Bang, they have remained so, separate from the darkness of the plasma. This light is still in evidence in the form of the cosmic microwave background radiation.

Perhaps not so obviously, the three other words beside the light (האור) and the darkness (החשך) in this phrase stand out: ויבדל (separated), בין

(between) and וּבֵין (and between). They are each serving as aspects of the forces generating duality in our world and they are the instruments of *Elokim*. "Separating" and "between" are two conceptual emblems that are completely consistent with the generation of contrast and, hence, duality. Separation by means of being made distinct is a pervasive principle in the account of Creation and, of course, it persists in our mundane human world as well. We will see "between" again shortly when the *rakiya* comes into existence. This oppositional contrast is an essential state woven into the fabric of the universe. It is not bad or wrong or something that needs to pass away or be rectified. Were there to be no separation and no position of "between," all would dissolve back into God's oneness again. Separation and opposition are musts in the process of Creation and the unfolding of the manifestations of duality for the sake of a binary world. The *tzimtzum* is still present and operating to generate the conditions that bring about the advent of "something" and "not-the-something" for the sake of producing an unfolding world of duality.

The created world is made of the following contrasting pairs: *yin* and *yang*, the two *hyule*, heaven and earth, *tohu v'vohu*, fire and water, the *Ein Sof* and the *tzimtzum*, light and darkness, Good and Evil. I once said to a class of students while I was teaching about the nature of *yin* and *yang*, not realizing that I was putting my foot in my mouth while attempting to be profound, "We live in a bipolar universe. There are no two ways about it."

CHAPTER ELEVEN

YOM ECHAD: FIFTH VERSE, FIRST CONCEIT

בְּרֵאשִׁית (בְּרֵאשִׁית) בָּרָא אֱלֹקִים אֵת הַשָּׁמַיִם וְאֵת הָאָרֶץ.
וְהָאָרֶץ הָיְתָה תֹהוּ וָבֹהוּ וְחֹשֶׁךְ עַל פְּנֵי תְהוֹם וְרוּחַ אֱלֹקִים
מְרַחֶפֶת עַל פְּנֵי הַמָּיִם. וַיֹּאמֶר אֱלֹקִים יְהִי אוֹר וַיְהִי אוֹר. וַיַּרְא
אֱלֹקִים אֶת הָאוֹר כִּי טוֹב וַיַּבְדֵּל אֱלֹקִים בֵּין הָאוֹר וּבֵין הַחֹשֶׁךְ.
וַיִּקְרָא אֱלֹקִים לָאוֹר יוֹם וְלַחֹשֶׁךְ קָרָא לָיְלָה וַיְהִי עֶרֶב וַיְהִי בֹקֶר
יוֹם אֶחָד.

FIRST CONCEIT

וַיִּקְרָא אֱלֹקִים.
God called or God called to or God named.

This phrase is subject to three different possible interpretations. Either it is "God called" or it is "God called to" or "God named." According to Rabbi Avraham Ibn Ezra, the meaning of this is "God named." Along the way in explaining this choice, the following rationale is used. God gave the light and the darkness names. As described in Genesis, Adam gave names to the various objects of the world (discrete created entities of all sorts, particularly the animals). As the state of things at this point in the narrative of the first *yom* precedes Adam coming into being, it is God that is giving names to the light and the darkness. It is axiomatic that once a name is given by God, it is a permanent label.

91

The act of calling produces an identity between what is called and the thing itself. The act of using a linguistic descriptor in the act of calling links the descriptor and the created entity itself. This is, in spite of a contrary opinion from the Ramban, an act of naming, as Ibn Ezra says. The naming of *ohr* and *choshech* as *yom* and *laylah*, respectively, establishes boundaries and limits on them, as they are now changed in the very act of their being named. This is consistent with the stepping down of the acts of creation into more and more physical forms. Clearly the act of naming establishes a new reality and makes or forms something new from previously existing things.

CHAPTER TWELVE

YOM ECHAD: FIFTH VERSE, SECOND CONCEIT

בְּרֵא שִׁית (בראשית) בְּרֵא אלקים אֵת הַשָּׁמַיִם וְאֵת הָאָרֶץ.
וְהָאָרֶץ הָיְתָה תֹהוּ וָבֹהוּ וְחֹשֶׁךְ עַל פְּנֵי תְהוֹם וְרוּחַ אלקים
מְרַחֶפֶת עַל פְּנֵי הַמָּיִם. וַיֹּאמֶר אלקים יְהִי אוֹר וַיְהִי אוֹר. וַיַּרְא
אלקים אֵת הָאוֹר כִּי טוֹב וַיַּבְדֵּל אלקים בֵּין הָאוֹר וּבֵין הַחֹשֶׁךְ.
וַיִּקְרָא אלקים לָאוֹר יוֹם וְלַחֹשֶׁךְ קָרָא לַיְלָה וַיְהִי עֶרֶב וַיְהִי בֹקֶר
יוֹם אֶחָד.

SECOND CONCEIT

(ו)יִּקְרָא (אלקים) לָאוֹר יוֹם וְלַחֹשֶׁךְ קָרָא לַיְלָה.
God named the light yom and named the darkness laylah.

On its own, this verse does not clarify what a *yom* is, and there are differing opinions from our Sages as to what the meaning could be. This is true of the need for clarification of what the meaning of *laylah* is as well. The narrative does not describe a conventional twenty-four-hour day like that produced by one full rotation of our planet on its axis as it revolves around our sun, since no physical sun or earth existed at this point. Therefore, we are bereft of our ability to conclude that our day of today is that *yom* in this verse. Or, that that *laylah* is our night. Reading ahead a trifle to the concluding phrase in this verse, we get to "*va'yehi erev va'yehi voker, yom echad.*" It is totally natural to assume that as long as our own clearly obvious, observable morning follows evening, and our night follows day, this verse in which *ohr* and *choshech* are being named is also giving us a sequence in time. I believe that this is not what this verse is indicating. The best we can do with unequivocal accuracy is say that *yom* and *laylah* are designations of interlinked, opposite, and complementary states. They may be akin to but not identical with stages in a progression.

We are naturally drawn to the conclusion that we are dealing with a description of temporal periodicity from the simple interpretation of this verse. However, since duality, obviously, prevails in this domain as well and we are looking to produce a more mystical unveiling, this interpretation will fall short of our needs. So, the nature of this statement is that it is an exposition of the drilling down into a more detailed texture of the manifesting universe. Time arises together with space, as the Ramban states and Einstein so ably proved mathematically. However, we are not able to assign any referenced, relative units of measure for time itself, since we are in an unknowable frame of reference. Therefore, assigning a number value to whatever designated units are found within one *yom* (as well as *laylah*) is not a winning approach or, perhaps, even a valid endeavour.

To this point in the text there is nothing with which to compare **this** *yom* and *laylah*. To determine the duration of these two periods is speculative. Added to that, here I point out that, physically, no sun and no earth means there are no twenty-four hours such as can be counted on the clock on the wall in my kitchen or from the relentless tick of a cesium atom-driven atomic clock. It remains inscrutable and impenetrable, since we cannot determine what units to use nor where the boundaries of measure should begin and end.

What we can say with certainty is that *ohr* and *yom* are linked through naming from God, and *choshech* and *laylah* are as well. This naming is, at minimum, due to a mere associative relationship as a function of the verb root word *kra* (קרא), as in *yikra* (יקרא). This is so whether the verb in this context means "called," "called to," or "named." Regardless of which meaning is most fitting, there is an associative connection as a function of the action of the verb root of *yikra* (יקרא) itself. This is also due to the juxtapositioning in the text and the flow of meaning in the narrative. In any case, since the application of any means of applying units of measure for *yom* (and *laylah*) is a hypothetical exercise, what we might have to say about it will have to be placed in the domain of the epilogue.

For the remainder of our discussion of the verse we are going to utilize the definitions and interpretations available to us through the work of Samson Raphael Hirsch on the etymology of Hebrew word roots. We will be relying on the *Etymological Dictionary of Biblical Hebrew* by Matityahu Clark. Of most interest is our analysis of the meaning-related individual words *ohr*, *yom*, and *boker* and the also meaning-related words *choshech*, *laylah*, and *erev*.

Through the word roots, let's revisit *ohr* and *choshech* using Rabbi Hirsch's work. The Hebrew letters here in parentheses are the three-letter word roots for *ohr* (אור) and *choshech* (חשׁך). By the account he gives, *ohr* is, indeed, light. Further and in addition, it is "shining," "gives light," and can even be "blinding." Among the definitional guidance he gives us, we find that much of what we know of *ohr* from the root word is found through its effects and it is reasonable, as said much earlier, to identify this *ohr* with the entire spectrum of electromagnetic radiation. We must carefully note here that the nature of all electromagnetic energy is that it is only recognizable when matter is present as its foil to be acted upon. This is inherent in the understanding that has flowed from the Heisenberg uncertainty principle. When one single electron is being measured and its exact position is being established, the velocity of its transit is altered, simply by the act of observing and measuring it. If the velocity is being measured, the exact position cannot be established; the observer affects the observed. Therefore, using the tools of *yin* and *yang* regarding *ohr*, it is clear that we are dealing with a *yang* energy force (active and activating). To wrap the previous verses together with this understanding, we have the following congruencies: fire, heaven, *tohu*, *yom*, [*boker* (coming soon)] and *yang*. While they are not synonymous, each is, nevertheless, linked and of the same valence or inner nature as the others.

This is also true of *choshech*, about which Rabbi Hirsch gives the descriptive terms "darken," "deprive of light," "darkening," and "obscuring." In spite of our usual treatment of *choshech* as a noun, the root word for it gives us action-oriented terms instead. For this word root, he assigned only verbs or words indicating influences to guide us. This is, nevertheless, not inconsistent with the effects that matter produces insofar as density, mass, etc., are interruptive to different states of electromagnetic energy, etc. A prime example of this is the state of the universe before photons uncoupled from matter, about which we spoke earlier, in which matter held the *ohr* captive, so to speak. As with *ohr*, I'm presenting a compilation of terms that also show congruence: water, earth, *bohu*, *laylah*, [*erev* (also coming soon)] and *yin*. In the context in which these terms first appear, they are linked in an opposite yet complementary relationship with their counterparts. There is internal consistency of these terms of a *yin* quality with each other, just as there is with the correspondents in the list in the paragraph above having to do with *ohr*. Here, too, while they are not synonymous, they are, nevertheless, linked due to being of the same valence or inner nature as each other.

Now, what is *yom*? The simple, commonplace reference definition or meaning for this word is "day." However, what is a day when there is no sun or moon? There are no planets, constellations, galaxies, or even any barely organized gas clouds in the expanding and still blisteringly hot universe at this point. It surely cannot be what we think of immediately when we say to another person, "Have a nice day," or when we think about Tuesday of next week, nor can it be the scientifically defined twenty-four-plus hours' span on standard modern timepieces. In any case, explicitly, I ask that we take it that *ohr* and *choshech* are paired and *yom* and *laylah* are also paired. This permits me some latitude to interpolate meanings and intents from the text.

The meaning I am choosing to take from Rabbi Hirsch about the three Hebrew letters that form the root word for *yom* is "ascend." In addition, he gives us "time of alertness," and through what is termed a gradational variant [יממ], "be clear." Although it may be somewhat questionable in this study of *yom* to do so, we are going to look into the nature of the word "ascend" and its derivatives, using Roget's Thesaurus:

Ascend (verb): 1) to move from a lower to a higher position: arise, climb, lift, mount, rise, soar; 2) To move upward on or along, climb, go up, mount, scale; 3) To attain a higher status, rank or condition: advance, climb, mount, rise.

Ascendance (noun): The condition or fact of being dominant: ascendancy, dominance, domination, parmountcy, predominance, preeminence, preponderancy, prepotency, supremacy.

Ascendant (adjective): Having preeminent significance: dominant, predominant, prepotent, prevailing, regnant, ruling supreme.

Ascendant (noun): A person from whom one is descended: mother, parent, progenitor.

Ascension (noun): 1) The act of rising or moving upward: ascent, rise, rising; 2) The act of moving upward on or along: ascent; climb.

Parsing out the duplicated definitions and synonyms, we are left with:

Ascend (verb): 1) to move from a lower to a higher position: arise, climb, lift, mount, rise, soar; 2) To move upward on or along, climb, go up, mount, scale; 3) To attain a higher status, rank or condition: advance.

Ascendance (noun): The condition or fact of being dominant: dominance, parmountcy, preeminence, preponderancy, prepotency, supremacy.

Ascendant (noun): A person from whom one is descended: ancestor, antecedent, father, forebear, forefather, foremother, mother, parent, progenitor.

Further distilling the remainder, the gist is this: The essence is of a rising up, of an ascension, an advancement on a scale, attaining a higher status. It is also of a preeminent nature, dominant in its place. It is also an antecedent, something that precedes and generates those that follow. From the Torah text, this *yom* is a cardinal number, declaring its existence in a state of primacy, rather than an ordinal number describing its order in a group.

We can turn to Kabbalah and discuss a brief and quite cursory overview of the ten *sefirot*. Of the ten *sefirot* (emanations of Divine light from the *Ein Sof* into Creation) the final or "bottom-most" one is *malchut* (kingship). The first of the *sefirot* is *keter* (crown). In the most common graphical displays of the *sefirot*, *keter* is at the top and *malchut* is at the bottom. As *keter* is considered "closest" to God Himself, *malchut* would be "further away." The diagram on the right is a typical graphical representation of the array of the sefirot.

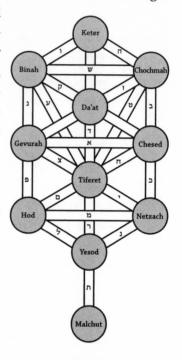

However, there is a stunning paradox at work here. As *malchut* is the last and, therefore, the completing and finalizing element of the array of the *sefirot*, it is, simultaneously, the original basis for the process. This is akin to the process of shooting an arrow at a target. One doesn't shoot the arrow and then look for the target. The target is acquired first and then the arrow is sent along the trajectory to find its way there. *Malchut*, then, is both the first and last of the *sefirot* to be "in mind" in the procession of the emanations from the light of the *Ein Sof*. Thus, the last is the first and the first is the last. This paradox is inherent in Creation and can be found again in the phrase I cited earlier about the creation of the Sabbath: "Last in deed but first in thought." In Kaplan's *Sefer Yetzirah* rendition, he says in relation to this, "The Sabbath is then the center point, which binds all together and supports them all. The Sabbath thus represents *malchut*, but in the mode in which it is bound to *keter*."

This exposition of the *sefirot* is prefatory to the understanding that the emanation of the light of the *Ein Sof* has two natures. It is both a declination of the brilliance of the light, dimming progressively through stages as it scales down from the edge of the *challal* into and then ter-minating at the center of it. Simultaneously, it is a rising up from the center to fill the *challal* with light.

The following is a reiteration of a passage from chapter 5: All of spir-itual and physical Creation is constructed using the *kav ohr Ein Sof*. The Ari describes the nature of the *kav*:

> *He then drew a simple concentrated ray from the Infinite light into the vacated space. The upper extremity of this ray touched the infinite light of Ein Sof that surrounded the space (the challal) and extended toward its center. It was through this ray, serving as a conduit, that the light of Ein Sof was brought down to spread into the entire vacated space.*

The speck that was brought into existence at the onset of Creation and from which the entire universe then expanded can reasonably be equated with the *sefirah* of *malchut*. If this is also equivalent to the Shettiah Stone (אבן שתייה or אבן שתיה) in ancient Jerusalem, it is also the place from which the entire universe was founded and expanded. As a function of those associations, the light brought down through the *challal* to the seat of *malchut* also ascended from there to fill the entire universe. Once "arriving" to the Shettiah Stone, it rose by seven progressive *yamim* to fill the *challal* with the universe. These *yamim* are the generations of *yamim* coming after the *yom* designated with a car-dinal number, *yom echad*. The narrative declares *yom echad*'s existence as a state of primacy. Those that follow are designated with ordinal numbers, describing their order in a group.

To further our discussion, the indications about the word *yom*, from the terms that Rabbi Hirsch gives are: rising up, an ascension, an advancement on a scale, attaining a higher status. Also, it is of a preeminent nature, dominant in its place. As well, it is an antecedent, something that precedes and generates those that follow. This is a de-scription, taken as a whole, of the primal singular origin of the emana-tion of the light of the *Ein Sof* as it arrives at and then expands from the center of the *challal*, in the progressions (of which there are seven) that are required to fill the *challal* with the now stepped-down-but-able-to-be-magnified power of the light. Here we return to the geometry of the *challal* as a perfect sphere, whose inherent number is seven, which now reappears in the manifesting of the stages of Creation called *yamim*, of which there are seven.

This beginning of the expansion of the light of the *Ein Sof* that now emanates from the center of the *challal* is certainly primal, original, and preeminent. As well, it is the ancestor of all of the light in the world, as it rises back to its Source, reaching for the limits for which Creation was created. This is for it to attain its higher status within the space that was created with the first *bet* of the Torah. *Yom echad* is the establishment of the one unique beginning: *b'reishit*. Each transformation of the light that takes place after this and over the following six *yamim* is preparing the way for the next one, ascending with each one, up to the creation of Man and Woman in their proper place with their highest status in all of Creation. At this juncture, we can accept that Adam and Chavah (Adam and Eve) were the two for whom the universe was made and within which their role is always to ascend to reach for their Creator.

Of course, *yom* is one portion of a two-member condition. The other portion is *laylah*. According to Rabbi Hirsch, the root word for *laylah* (לול) means "blend together." In addition, he goes on to designate "night" and "time when everything is mixed." This term is indicative of a state wherein things are intermixed and confounded. Basically, distinctiveness is a cross-language antonym to *laylah*.

This is congruent with the natures of *yin* and *yang*, insofar as, for example, *yin* is murky (dark) and *yang* is clear (bright). Also, light is *yang* and darkness is *yin*, as the symbol shows. This symbol also shows the directionality of the inter-transformational natures of *yin* and *yang*, generated by movement in the clockwise direction of the implied motion. *Yin* descends, *yang* ascends. We go from upright during the day, a *yang* position, to lying down, a *yin* state, at night. And, of course, the reverse is true as we rise up again with the dawning of a new day.

In the discussion of *yom* in his Torah commentary, Rabbi Hirsch relates *yom* (יום) to the word *kavam* (קום), which we have already encountered in chapter 5 in the discussion involving Psalm 19: "Their line (קום) goes forth throughout the earth..." Rabbi Hirsch says, "To light He assigned day, *yom* (יום) related to *kavam* (קום), when everything rises to independence and stands independently...During the day, man stands upright."[31] The root of the word קום is *kav* (קו), and the footnote to the passage in Psalms says the following, "*Their line.* The precision of the universe is likened metaphorically to a surveyor's tape (*tohu*) stretched out to the ends of the earth. This means that the precision of the cosmos is evident all over the earth to any observer." Clearly, for such precision to be evident to any observer, it must be *yom* with the immediacy of its correlation with light, organizing forces, and *yang* (uprightness, verticality).

The terms *yom* and *laylah* are the indicated names produced by association with *ohr* and *choshech*. The light that is referenced at this point, although already in its stepped-down intensity, had no source like the sun or another star, as it is the descendent of the original light from the third verse. Remember that in Hebrew, this *ohr* (אור) has no physical source from which it emanates (מ'אור), like the sun or stars. This *ohr* (אור) is still the primordial light to which the third, fourth, and fifth verses in the Torah refer. The remnants of this light which now comprise the so-called cosmic microwave background radiation, were in the process of cooling at this point in the Torah narrative into which we are delving.

The *choshech*, too, is a stepped-down or diluted version of its former self. This is so as a function of the evolving nature of Creation. Less abstract and more concretized which, counterintuitively, means that it is **less** dense than the original created darkness. Regardless of the degree to which we encounter *choshech* as a dense created reality, it still remains opposite of the light. From a *yin/yang* perspective, light is relatively *yang* and darkness is relatively *yin*. As a brief refresher, *yin* is

---

31   Samson Raphael Hirsch, *The Hirsch Chumash* (Jerusalem: Feldheim, 2002), vol. I, p. 13.

concretizing and centripetal, dense, and sinks to the center. And *yang* is its opposite. In Rabbi Hirsch's commentary, the earlier notated quotation is followed by "...darkness to night; לילה, root לול from which we get לולאות dragging along, the time when everything sinks down, and the whole world is lying down and no longer stands there in its own separate outline."

For the purposes of our exploration, the essence of the ideas associating light and *yom* come from the descriptions given by Rabbi Hirsch. They are then being combined with the discussions of light mostly found in chapter 8 and beyond. Hirsch's description of *yom* as "ascend," with its attendant meanings added to it as shown above, gives us a rising up, an ascension, an advancement on a scale, attaining a higher status. Also, it is of a preeminent nature, dominant in its place. As well, it is an antecedent, something that precedes and generates those that follow of its own kind. This description places these characteristics in the realm of being shaping forces. This is also, therefore, directed by the citation to Psalm 19, akin to *tohu* and calls up the corresponding other terms that anchor our discussion and understanding.

The general sense of *yom* is, therefore, clear, standing up, where everything rises to its own independence, the time of being erect, alert, and with ascension. The flavor of *laylah* is that everything is indistinct, confounded, without its own separate outline. This description of *laylah* is highly reminiscent of *bohu*. *Bo hu*; it is in it. What is the "it" that is in it? Everything, merely undifferentiated. With the advent of the light, order and organization are imposed on the darkness, and then the multiplicity of the world springs into existence, now distinguished out. The manifesting universe is progressing further along in increments toward its ultimate realization.

We now have our opposite and yet complementary paired terms once again. We can conclude that these two terms, *yom* and *laylah*, are features of the process of the measurement of time. This is supported by the simplest meanings of the words day and night. However, the units and the standard for those units are, nevertheless, undisclosed and unobtainable. Speculations can be raised as to exactly how much time has passed once we get to the final letter of the fifth verse. However, this is indeterminate and subject to conjecture.

Instead, we've now progressed through a number of transformations from the advent of Creation as it works through the process of producing a home for conscious, reflective human beings. They too are reflections of duality with physical bodies for existence and spirit able to contemplate their origins and their Creator.

CHAPTER THIRTEEN

YOM ECHAD:
FIFTH VERSE,
THIRD CONCEIT

ברא שית (בראשית) ברא אלקים את השמים ואת הארץ.
והארץ היתה תהו ובהו וחשך על פני תהום ורוח אלקים
מרחפת על פני המים. ויאמר אלקים יהי אור ויהי אור. וירא
אלקים את האור כי טוב ויבדל אלקים בין האור ובין החשך.
ויקרא אלקים לאור יום ולחשך קרא לילה ויהי ערב ויהי בקר
יום אחד.

THIRD CONCEIT

ויהי ערב ויהי בקר יום אחד.

And there was erev and there was boker, one yom ("yom one"
or "yom [of the] one)."

The following are excerpts from Rabbi Samson Raphael Hirsch's Torah commentary and Clark's *Etymological Dictionary of Biblical Hebrew*, based on the writings of Hirsch.

From the etymology as compiled by Matityahu Clark:

> **Erev (ערב)**—*Mix substances with no change in character; (1)*
> *mixing without being integrated; (2) darkening; (5) evening;*
> *mixed shades of light; (6) twilight*

Boker **(בקר)**—*Distinguishing difference; (1) examining; (4) morning; time of distinguishing*[32]

From Rabbi Hirsch's Torah commentary, cited above:

> *The commencement of each of these times (yom and laylah) is boker (בקר) and erev (ערב) [respectively]. Erev (ערב) where the two conditions begin to mix, and boker (בקר) related to בכר, בגר, פקר—to be free, independent, where things separate from each other and appear in their own outline and it is already possible לבקר, to distinguish one from the other.*

As we're drilling down into more esoteric meanings, since neither earth nor sun has existence yet, Hirsch's interpretations are extremely valuable. We have to get past the simple meaning (*p'shat*), which is such a lure, having us believe that the narrative is describing the sun rising and setting on our earth in this verse. This dilemma also exists for the following two days as well, *yom sheini* (second) and *yom shlishi* (third). Until the fourth *yom*, there are no celestial or planetary bodies which can have mornings and evenings. The *Zohar*, from the Soncino Press, says:

> *R. Eleazar then began thus: Consider this: [...] The Holy One, blessed be He, created the world in six days and each day revealed a part of His work, and functioned through the energy imparted to it. But none of the work was actually disclosed nor the energy functioning until the fourth day. The first three days were undisclosed and imperceptible, but when the fourth day came, the product and energy of all of them was brought out in the open.*

In the first few *yamim*, the world is being prepared for our earth and sun to produce evenings and mornings, with darkness and light. Our view of our surroundings is confounded as the day darkens and then is liberated while a new day dawns with discrete things appearing.

---

32   Pp. 30, 191.

We are pursuing the predecessor conditions that are of the essence of the creative forces and materials at work. Therefore, the references found in Hirsch's writings and Clarks' compilations of them bring us to certain conclusions. The *erev* and the *boker* spoken of at the conclusion of the fifth verse of the Torah are declaring and drawing some phase of Creation to an intended demarcation point. This point in the manifestation of the universe is singular and unique. It is of a preeminent nature, dominant in its place. As well, it is the antecedent that precedes and generates the six *yamim* that follow it.

Obviously, since *erev* and *boker* are opposites, they conform to the idea that the whole universe is a construct that is consistent with the frame of duality, consistent with the archetypes of *yin* and *yang*. A condition of mixing (and being undistinguished) is *yin*, and distinguishing differences is *yang*. Further, this is a culmination of sorts for all of the paired opposites of duality coming into some focus from an otherwise indeterminate status. In his rendition of *Sefer Yetzirah*, Aryeh Kaplan discusses the links between fire and heaven and water and earth when he says on page 147, "heaven is created from fire" and "earth is created from water." Here they are in visual display, on a relative basis, the left column being *yang* and the right column *yin*:

Creator	created
one	two
hyule of heaven	*hyule* of earth
heaven	earth
aish	*mayim*
tohu	*bohu*
ohr	*choshech*
yom	*laylah*
boker	*erev*

Before we leave *yom echad* and anticipate *yom sheini*, I have to strongly note the matter of the paradoxical nature of time and of cause and effect which permeates it. On the one hand, what you've read so far stands firmly for the simultaneity of so many of the distinctions noted in the text. Yet, there is, arguably, some kind of progression along a path of change. For example, the nature of the *rakiya*, to which virtually the entire *yom sheini* is devoted, is a clear necessity for *erev* and *boker* to remain distinct as separate elements of Creation. This includes that it is brought into existence to change the nature of the water from "earlier" in the first *yom*. It almost seems that the *rakiya* reaches back from the *yom sheini* to interact with something that we have left behind in the narrative many paragraphs before. These concerns about simultaneity and cause and effect are particularly relevant once the luminaries themselves are fashioned on the fourth *yom*, for then we will have our planetary home and the sun.

The mystery of Creation must, of necessity, be out of our grasp and whatever stabs at certainty we've exposed in the chapters until now are really questionable, relative certainties at that. In the end, the paradoxes of Creation that arise due to the insistence of the chain of cause and effect so inherent in our universe when juxtaposed with the simultaneity of the earliest micro-moments of Creation must remain our very human conundrum. When we contextualize the narrative of the first two *yamim* from God's perspective, wherein no time or space exists, we must ultimately scratch our collective heads in wonder; we are teased with what seems the dawning light of possibility for understanding and knowledge of Creation, only to recognize in the end that what we encounter that draws us to think we know fades like a phantom in the face of God's unfathomable brilliance.

Of course, all of duality is ultimately an expression of the will of the Creator, having been generated by the act of creating "creating" and the act of creating the *challal* itself, generated from the *tzimtzum* wherein God withdrew Himself from Himself. We are now about to crystallize the duality of Creation, as the light rises up successively to its fullest. This permits conscious, reflective human beings who can embody and live within the operational, everyday duality of good and evil. Crucially, this includes the ability within human beings to choose either good or evil with complete freedom. Now, the second *yom* awaits, for the consummation of the advent of duality has yet to take place and become fixed. Without the *rakiya*, it could all revert to oneness again.

CHAPTER FOURTEEN

YOM SHEINI: FIRST VERSE, FIRST CONCEIT

ויאמר אלקים יהי רקיע בתוך המים ויהי מבדיל בין מים למים. ויעשׂ אלקים את הרקיע ויבדל בין המים אשר מתחת לרקיע ובין המים אשר מעל לרקיע ויהי כן. ויקרא אלקים לרקיע שמים ויהי ערב ויהי בקר יום שני.

FIRST VERSE

ויאמר אלקים יהי רקיע בתוך המים ויהי מבדיל בין מים למים.

In the Ramban's Torah commentary, in relation to the *rakiya* and its role in Creation, he writes,

> *This is one of the subjects of the account of Creation, so do not expect me to write anything about it! For the matter is one of the hidden mysteries of the Torah, and the verses do not require any such elaboration, for Scripture does not go to any length in this matter, and elaboration is forbidden to those who understand it, and all the more so to us!*

With this warning in mind and with concerns for the validity of the exposition that follows, I'm going to begin, nevertheless, to make a set of firm assertions as we untangle the mystery of the *rakiya*. This entire second *yom* is devoted to the description of this most inscrutable term and its impact and import in the unfolding duality that is Creation. In summary and as preface, without the *rakiya*, the entire enterprise of Creation would be subject to reversion to the former states of indistinctness and chaos. The power of *Elokim* in generating the forces of distinction and separateness essential to a universe of multiplicity is undeniable. That said, as I maintained earlier, without some means of perpetuating the distinctions in an ongoing fashion, while continually renewing the account of Creation, all would revert to God's oneness again, and nothing would have duration in order for time and space to come into existence and then persist and evolve.

The second *yom*, as I said at the very beginning, and its partner, *yom echad*, comprise the critical engagement of what was required to have a universe in which God's purpose, including our individual and collective missions as free-willed beings, could be fulfilled. Duality is established by the declarations in the first two *yamim*. The second *yom*, with its elaboration on the *rakiya*, is the first state achieved in the unfolding distinctions in the account of Creation that generates the phrase "and it was so—*vayehi chein* (ויהי כן)." This is an essential requirement and turns out to be the mortar that holds the structure of duality together.

FIRST CONCEIT

ויאמר אלקים יהי רקיע.

And God said, "Let there be a rakiya."

Here is what Rabbi Hirsch describes (brought to us in this form by Matityahu Clark's book) as the meaning of this most enigmatic word:

> **Rakiya (רקע):** Crush; forcibly flatten
>
> (1) flattening; (2) establish firmly; (3) overlaying

As said before in relation to when God declares the advent of the light, we are again encountering a statement depicting the enactment of the will of God. Here, too, God is not speaking in any kind of way which we could describe in human terms. In any case, our Sages agree that this is descriptive of the will of God. As it is *Elokim* that utters this, it is a new distinction that is being declared into existence.

This is the second time that the ideational realm of God's creating is made explicit by His "giving voice" to a designation that establishes a new distinction. God has again altered His relationship with His Creation. As with the declaration bringing the light into existence, this change generates an enormous transformation in the formulation of Creation henceforward. Here we have another differentiation of immense significance. The nature of the *rakiya* is being established and imposed on the already existing status of Creation. All that being said, we are still left with the question: So what **is** the *rakiya*?

Some of the most common interpretations assigned to the word *rakiya* are firmament, partition, sky, or expanse. Of those terms, none of which I believe really hit the center of the target, partition seems to be most relevant to our understanding here. However, there is nary a commentary that goes much beyond any of these terms to delve into and then reveal what **principle** is operating as the *rakiya* is invoked. At this point in the narrative, the fundamental substances that we find named in the periodic table of the elements, like chlorine or silicon or uranium, don't exist yet. Only with the completion of the second *yom* **can** a physical world come into existence, and then persist. Only then, after that, can stars ignite and planets form. While the stars and planets are the province of the fourth *yom*, the conditions generated by the second *yom* (and, of course, the third as well) are essential to the progression that produces solar systems. Once this second *yom* is complete, the building of the actual structures that make life possible can begin. The evolving transformations of the powers, forces, and substances that have been generated can become the physical and energetic building blocks of a viable universe.

I believe the most fitting interpretation for the *rakiya*, contextually, abstractly, and finally, physically, is that it is the Principle of Division for the whole universe. What this means is that with the generation of the *rakiya*, God brings into being the agent for persistence in distinguishing and separation. As an abstract principle, it is completely independent of space and time. Hence, we find the expression "and it was so" for the

first time in the Torah. This statement is widely considered to be a declaration of permanence; the crucial step in the process of establishing
duality perpetually.

The *rakiya* separates and contains, but it is not in any way a physical
structure. Yet, it provides the template for all of the emerging, discrete
physical structures required for a functional universe which are distinctly separate phenomena. One could say that the *rakiya* is an abstract yet
organizational force generating the agency for persistence of division
and separation. This is consistent with the very essence of duality and is
clearly congruent with the power of *Elokim* to make things distinct and
separate. The principle of separating and segregating is something that
is emblematic of and flows naturally from the Power Above All Powers
(*Elokim*). Thus, this agent, the *rakiya*, is what stands behind the making
of anything distinct which had not previously been so. This making of
something distinct can then exist on a persistent and perpetual basis.
In addition, it is characteristic of and a clear manifestation of God's
attribute of *El Shakkai* (אל שקי).[33]

This essential nature of the Sovereign of the universe holds sway over
nature. This power is exemplified by the restraint God placed on His
expanding world by simply uttering the word "enough." This generates,
establishes, and implements the epitome of limits and the power of
boundary-setting. Thus, we have a virtual equivalency, in quality, of
Elokim, *El Shakkai*, and the *rakiya*. This internal consistency shows the
complete congruence of the forces at work in the initial shaping of our
world. We find the result of this in a universe filled with multiplicity.
However, that multiplicity is born of duality.

If we were to apply physical terms of measurement to analyze the
rakiya, given the root word for it, we must be dealing with something
exceedingly thin. In *Talmud Chagigah* 15a, it is variously described as no
wider than three fingersbreadth thick, or a hairsbreadth, or as thin as
the space between two identical teacups, one stuck inside the other, etc.
This abstract principle is the template for what we are about to encounter

---

33 This word, being one of God's holy names, is written and pronounced with a ד (*dalet*) in the
place of the ק (*qof*) when used in a prayer or scriptural text.

in the next portion of this verse. Applying this "measurement" in other ways, we can begin to inspect the history of, as well as the current state of, the universe, for evidence of its existence. In chapter 15, the next phrase in this verse leads us to the first "physical" appearance of the *rakiya* and its role in the newly birthed advent of existence.

In the meantime, the very principle of separation and containment, which I more briefly term "limits and boundaries," clearly shown in earlier chapters, is a required element of a duality world created by *Elokim*. Also, as said earlier, without this capability woven into the very fabric of existence, all would simply revert to unity, and God would have no Creation at all. The implications of this have ramifications throughout everything that is relevant to human beings everywhere and every-when. For example, for those of us who have or have had children who are quite young, we know the necessity of limits and boundaries for them. Without such constraints, children are likely to endanger themselves or others, or act like little animals, generating havoc wherever they go. This example, obviously, belongs to the domain of the psychosocial. However, all diverse aspects of Creation fall under its sway as well. We'll have more to explore as I go through this singularly devoted *yom* and its elucidation of the *rakiya*.

The vast majority of Torah commentators regard the second *yom* as having sown the seeds of *machloket* (discord), as it is a period during which separation and division occurs and in which the word *tov* (good) is not to be found in the narrative. The reason for this is that, viewed through a familiar lens, opposition is bad. Disputes, conflict, and human strife all arise from *machloket*. On the other hand, from within the confines of our discussion in this work, opposition is **essential** for the unfolding of Creation. This is reflected in an earlier citation from Michael L. Munk, found on page 26 in this work, having to do with the necessity of contrast (of black and white) for creating a multi-discrete world. Nevertheless, given the dangers of *machloket*, please refer to the final comments on division and separation toward the very end of chapter 21.

It is also strikingly similar to God's having created evil, which we discussed in chapter 2. The synergy of opposites and their mutual complementarity, including their interdependent and inter-transformational relationship, all generate a natural, mutual counterbalance of forces. Later in Genesis, we see Adam requiring a helpmate *k'negdo* (opposite) him. Eve was the result. Surely the Torah isn't telling us that God wanted a mate for Adam so that they could have discord! The interplay of opposites yields dynamic, organic adaptability and change, which are inherent conditions required for the success of living things. The early chapters of this book are clear statements of duality being an absolutely critical fundamental in the design of our world. The second *yom* cements that feature into existence on a permanent basis. It is surely a fitting goodness for life.

If the *rakiya* is to be accorded fair rights to the title "(The) Principle of Division," it must be able to be found throughout the physical universe in multiple forms, shapes, and sizes, existing from some of the earliest moments in time to this very day. It must be able to be found woven into the very fabric of physical structures, as well as the natural processes of change in all dynamic systems. As I am discussing the principle of division and separation, perhaps it is best that we recognize examples for this that can be observed very near at hand in the external environment as well as within our own bodies (as well as within every other created thing: animal, vegetable, or mineral).

There is one single indispensable physical structure in all living things, without which there is literally no life or potential for life at all: membranes. Membranes are extremely thin. They envelop and separate structures in the bodies of all living creatures. This includes viruses. Membranes of varied types are found in all cells of every zoological creature and each cell of all botanical creatures. Surrounding each cell is the cell wall, a membrane. Whether it encloses, thereby defining the limits of, single-cell amoebas or cells in the pulp of a Redwood tree, the cell membrane is that structure without which cells could never be discrete. More striking, without the divisor of self and other that the cell membrane permits and generates, not one single-celled entity could have come into existence, much less lived to be able to propagate itself. Life itself is dependent on the existence of the cell membrane and, therefore, on the *rakiya*. By virtue of the generation of separateness, the distinctness of self and other comes into existence. Variable interchanges between and within dynamic systems are now possible.

The following are taken from two well-used members of a commonly populated library from a Jewish home: "He Who stretched out heaven like a thin membrane,"[34] derived from *Isaiah* 40:22, and, "Who spreads the heavens like a thin curtain, and stretches them like a tent to dwell in."[35] These two passages, both of which are taken from the writings of the prophet Isaiah, are representative of other descriptions that are relevant to our discussion. The essence of these passages is thinness and a stretched-out nature. These are the two basic qualities of the *rakiya*.

Given the above, the profusion of membranes in the human body is of dramatic importance. For example, there are membranes surrounding every organ and most structures of the body; brain, heart, stomach, every muscle group, etc. Those envelopes of tissue are largely made of collagen, which has unique properties. Collagen is electrically conductive, as it passes direct current (DC as opposed to AC) micro-currents of electricity along the lengths of its strands. In addition, it has the unusual capacity of actually generating electricity, as the crystalline structure of collagen fibers produces a piezoelectric effect. That is, they generate micro-currents of electricity when they are deformed and reformed to assume their former shape. Therefore, actually, we are each electrical conductors and generators. This property, resting as it does on the differential between negative and positive charges, reflects itself in other functions that we require in order to live. An example of this is found in the nature of human bones. It was discovered relatively recently that in passing micro-current direct (DC, not AC) current through what would otherwise be termed non-healing bone fractures, healing would be dramatically enabled and sped up. This technique allows two bone pieces to firmly cement together where there would otherwise have been no uniting of the fracture. This is due to the power of the collagen contained within the fascial membranes within our bones.

---

34   Nosson Scherman, *The Complete Artscroll Machzor Yom Kippur* (Brooklyn: Mesorah, 1986), pp. 390–391.

35   *Isaiah* 40:22. Scherman, *Tanach*, pp. 1022–1023.

For any given cell of our bodies we have a cell wall (membrane), vacuoles which transport substances into and out of the cell (which are enclosed by a membrane), mitochondria (segregated from the rest of the cell contents by a membrane), and the nucleus, which is also enclosed by a membrane. We're not going to discuss any of the other structures of the cell here. Further evidence for the *rakiya* in the body is found in the form of the diaphragm, the great dome of thin muscle stretched upward from its attachments at the bottom of the ribcage. The diaphragm separates the heart, lungs, and pericardium from the stomach, liver, spleen, intestines, kidneys, bladder, and in females, the ovaries and the uterus.

In Chinese medicine, the torso is divided into three sections. From the top of the torso at the collarbones to the level of the diaphragm is the upper portion. From the diaphragm to the level of the navel is the middle portion, and from the level of the navel to the bottom of the torso is the lower portion. More broadly, and very obviously, the diaphragm separates the region above the diaphragm from the region below the diaphragm. The region above the diaphragm is considered the realm of heaven, and the region below it is considered the realm of earth.

If one has ever observed a baby breathing, one can see that it is the diaphragm moving up and down, just like a bellows, which moves the breath, not the muscles of the chest wall. The rhythmic movement of the diaphragm causes the regularity of the respiratory rhythm, which itself regulates the rhythmicity of the heart. The diaphragm itself is a minimal thing, it being a membrane like others in the body (although considerably thicker than the others in the body), yet it causes movement. This is just like the electrical conductivity of the fascia with its constituency of collagen.

As we breathe air into our lungs, the oxygen in the inhaled air diffuses through the membranous structure of the tiny, delicate, filament-like branchlets of the air sacs. It is there that they meet the tiniest of capillaries of the vascular system, thereby dissolving the oxygen into the bloodstream. In return, the blood yields up its dissolved carbon dioxide, moving from the capillaries into the air sacs in the opposite direction to the oxygen, through the same membrane, then to be exhaled into the atmosphere. This power of the principle of division and separation is at work in us at least seventeen times every minute of every day on average. When we are healthy, it is truly inexhaustible. Contrariwise, the green, growing plants have exactly the opposite exchange, whereby they inspire CO_2 and exhale O_2. While plants don't have a diaphragm, they do have openings that permit the flow of gases in a respiratory rhythm that is complementary to ours.

Semi-permeable membranes are found within the kidneys, which have the ability to filter wastes and other substances from the blood. Certain molecules are small enough to fit through the tiny pore size of the filtering membrane, and larger ones are retained. As well, there's a pressure gradient across the membrane which forces certain substances out of the blood into the collecting tubules of the cortex of the kidneys' filtering structure. Additionally, the ionic composition of the dissolved salts (sodium, potassium, and calcium being most common here) govern the movement of ions across the membrane, including retaining those that are needed. How incredibly brilliant a design it all is.

When we look to the atmosphere of our earth, we find a different kind of *rakiya*. Many of our Sages, including the Ramban and the Malbim, consider the *rakiya* to be that part of the atmosphere where weather occurs. In my opinion, our weather zone, the troposphere, is not the *rakiya*. It shows us the region that abuts a *rakiya*. This section of the air on our planet is a perfect place to look for evidence of the **manifestation** of the *rakiya*. Earlier, I cited the fact that about fifty percent of the earth's surface water is in the oceans and seas and fifty percent of it is within the atmosphere in clouds, dissolved in the air as vapor or falling as rain or some form of frozen precipitation.

The region in which the transition of water vapor to liquid water to frozen water and back again is found between the surface of the earth and the troposphere. That is, it is the region of change within which variations of temperature and pressure will produce the transition from one state to another; appearing as either a solid, liquid, or a gas, all depending on interrelationship of temperature and pressure. From a physics perspective, this is governed by what is known as Boyle's law.

For example, at earth-bound atmospheric temperatures and pressures, the substance methane is a gas. On Saturn's moon, Titan, it's believed that methane is a liquid, having produced vast oceans of liquid methane due to the extreme cold and massive pressures, due to the gravity exerted on it from Saturn. The invisible divisor which creates phase transitions for molecules and atoms is often graphed in the way shown in the illustration at the end of this chapter.

One can see that the Y-axis is pressure and the X-axis is temperature. This graph shows the relationships of the phases of water in relation to each other, dependent on the variability according to temperature and pressure combinations. The important point here, however, is that these phases are separate and divided, fitting to the environment of earth. It should be quite clear that the phenomenon of phase transition is one of the *rakiya*'s expressions of the Principle of Division at work in our world, particularly on our earth. It can't be seen, measured, touched, tasted, smelled, or located in some physical place. Its operations are universal and govern the state of things in the physical world. It itself, however, is not physical. One might say it is metaphysical, a spiritual tool of the Almighty. This is a clearcut example of duality generating multiplicity.

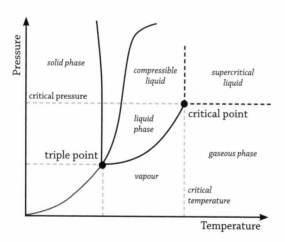

CHAPTER FIFTEEN

YOM SHEINI: FIRST VERSE, SECOND CONCEIT

ויאמר אלקים יהי רקיע בתוך המים ויהי מבדיל בין מים למים. ויעשׂ אלקים את הרקיע ויבדל בין המים אשר מתחת לרקיע ובין המים אשר מעל לרקיע ויהי כן. ויקרא אלקים לרקיע שמים ויהי ערב ויהי בקר יום שני.

SECOND CONCEIT

בתוך המים ויהי מבדיל בין מים למים.

[I]n the midst of the water(s) and let it separate between the water(s) and the water(s).

The word, *b'tōch* appears again in the account of the Garden of Eden after the seventh *yom*. There we see it in the phrase "the Tree of Life in the midst of the garden," once *Elokim* has completed His work (*v'etz ha'chaim b'tōch ha'gan*—ועץ החיים בתוך הגן). The consensus opinion is that "in the midst" means in the exact center: not near the center or in the region of the center, but the center of the bull's eye kind of center. Separating water from water? What are the results that doing so could produce? If this is the primeval or near-primeval state of things, mustn't we be in the plasma state of the universe? What effect would separating plasma from plasma produce? How can we know what this is coming to teach us?

First, we need to answer the question about the water(s) in which the *rakiya* is "placed" by God. What are our possibilities? Which water is it? Is this water the water of *aish* and *mayim* that comprises the initial reference to *shamayim* in the first verse of the Torah? Is it the water that describes the superheated, churning sea of subatomic particles winking in and out of existence from which the light was brought forth, that was the proto-matter/electromagnetic energy post Big Bang? Is it the water that is about to be collected into one place on the third *yom*? We have to know to where our progress through the narrative has brought us with this reference. The nature of the final components of Creation at this point is that they are immanent, not actually physically configured. Certainly, this *mayim* is not the water with which we are familiar today, as in the H_2O from our faucets or in streams and in oceans in which we can swim. This *mayim* is not those. Given our working definition of the Principle of Division for the *rakiya*, it behooves us to find the earliest medium which we can identify as water, through which the *rakiya* worked its effects. The labors of some of the most brilliant scientific minds in history have now granted us access to reliable evidence about the conditions in the earliest moments in the manifesting physical universe.

The position I am taking is that this *mayim* is, indeed, the superheated post Big Bang beginnings of matter and energy. Now, it may seem that we left this "stage" behind quite some time ago (chapters 7 and 8). However, the logical choice is to consider that we are still dealing here with the proto-matter and electromagnetic energy that appeared very shortly after the Big Bang took place. This was the state referred to as the quark-gluon plasma; the near-perfect liquid. That we seem to be going backward in time is due to the apparent linearity of the text. However, this is not a progression of linear time. Rather, we are again being shown different features of the just-manifesting abstractions that God used, leading to their immediate, short- and longer-term progressions into a more physical world.

As the plasma cooled, the power of division and separation began to generate certain distinctions. The four fundamental forces, the strong and weak forces, electromagnetism and gravity, separated from one another and began to become distinct. Also, the differentiation of matter and energy, dark matter and dark energy, matter and anti-matter, positively charged particles and negatively charged particles became distinct and began to show persistence. In order for these cosmological pairs to generate proper conditions for this universe, permanence was required from the Principle of Division and separation. As an example, a magnet has never been found or created that has a greater or lesser number than two magnetic poles with exactly equal power. Positive and negative electrical charges are equal. Protons (positively charged) and electrons (negatively charged), exist in equal numbers and paired sub-atomic particles, half with up-spin and half with down-spin are equal to each other in number. Many other examples abound that are of exactly equal composition. With matter and energy transforming into each other at the stage of this "water," energy and matter are in a dynamic mode of conserving their equality. The nature of the water in which the *rakiya* is placed is summed up in the simplest of equations: $E = mc^2$.

We find many pairs of opposites within the quark-gluon plasma: Electrons/positrons, particles with up-spin and particles with down-spin, etc. However, no doubt the most critical of all for the progression to a physical universe was the matter/anti-matter dichotomy. It was that distinctive state of tension that had to be divided and separated in such a way that a universe composed of matter was what ensued. According to accepted data, the number of particles of matter and the number of particles of anti-matter matched each other. How could it be otherwise? Actually, it was not quite equal. Science will tell us that statistically speaking, there were 1,000,000,000 particles of anti-matter for every 1,000,000,001 particles of matter. Of course, the members of both varieties would, once they were divided and separated from each other in order to be made distinct, annihilate each other in unfathomably enormous releases of energy on coming together again. However, one single particle of matter was left over from the collisions of one billion particles of anti-matter with one billion and one particles of matter. Those inconceivably huge numbers of trillions upon trillions of annihilations left us with all of the matter (and, therefore, energy) in our universe; truly an incomprehensibly staggering number to contemplate. The division in the "middle" of the seething mass of superheated plasma was accomplished because the *rakiya* was placed in the midst of it and divided and separated it into paired opposites. This description is completely congruent with everything we have laid out in previous chapters. The Rambam describes the division between the waters as an act of generating a distinction in nature or form.

As we are inevitably moving in the direction of more and more materiality, we are now going to look to the manifestations that have come into existence in our world. These are those from which we can extrapolate backward to the advent of the Principle of Division that is the *rakiya*. I can now refer us back to the discussions of our Sages mentioned earlier in this chapter, who determined that our own atmosphere was the *rakiya*. This is, however, a case in which **the** *rakiya* has **manifestations** that appear in the physical world. We can extrapolate this convention from the plasma down to the molecules of physical water that are inherently integral to life here on earth. By most estimates, as said earlier, the same amount of water in the form of snow, rain, ice, and vapor is found in the earth's atmosphere as liquid and frozen water is found in all of the earth's oceans, lakes, and rivers. As the sun beats down on the bodies of water, the electromagnetic energy of the photons agitates the water molecules of the liquid water and ice on the surface of the earth. As the molecules of water absorb that energy, they experience an increase in the stored kinetic energy (they heat up) to the point that they make the transition into water vapor (a gas).

While it may not be so obvious, this even happens in continually snow-covered or ice-covered regions. Recalling the phase transition chart shown in the last chapter, one can see that frozen water can go directly from a solid state to a gaseous state under the right conditions of temperature and pressure. One can readily see how this might take place by comparing this to dry ice (frozen carbon dioxide) as it "melts." Instead of melting into liquid carbon dioxide, when it thaws at temperatures and pressures in which we normally observe this phenomenon, it goes directly into the gaseous state. The milky-ness of the clouds that surround dry ice when it is leaving the solid state is due to the extreme cooling effect on the water vapor in the air being quickly super-cooled, thus making a little cloud like we would otherwise see in the sky.

As water vapor from the surface of the earth rises, it cools and forms clouds. Once enough vapor has come together to form a cloud, supersaturated with water, it will condense in the form of rain, snow, or hail. Sleet and freezing rain are caused by temperatures that are below freezing at lower altitudes than at the bottom of the cloud. Once precipitation falls, it will add to the snowpack or the ice caps or glaciers, or the oceans, seas, rivers, or streams. Once in solid or liquid version on the surface, it may again be agitated into the vapor state and rise up into the atmosphere to form new clouds to give us a new rainstorm or snow or hail. And, again, the cycle will recur, perpetually. The region between the surface and the atmosphere may be a gap that is actually no wider than a hairsbreadth or the space between two teacups that are stuck together. Whatever the distance may be between them, it is, nevertheless, the *rakiya* that equally divides the two, just as it says, "*b'tōch.*" From the *Midrash Rabbah*, "R' Yochanan said: On the second day of Creation, the Holy One, blessed is He, took all the waters that were in existence at the beginning of Creation and placed half of them [above] the firmament and half of them in the ocean."[36]

The *rakiya* operates in the cells during ordinary cell division. This is available for observation under the microscope while viewing a recently fertilized human egg. Recorded video footage can be found on the internet by searching for "cell division video" in a search engine. A single cell suddenly divides and separates into two identical cells. This process happens again and again, producing the geometric progression of numbers of cells going from 1 to 2 to 4, then 8, 16, 32, 64, 128, 256, 512, 1024, etc., doubling and redoubling over and over. This operating principle of division and separation enables the flourishing of animate growth. The resulting two cells from each division are identical morphologically in every way.

These divisions are taking place within the nucleus of the cell, during a process that's known as mitosis. Before the process of mitosis begins,

---

36   Blinder, *Midrash Rabbah* vol. I, ch. 4, p. 4.

the DNA found within the nucleus of the cell is a tangle of strands. At a certain moment, the strands thicken and double themselves into the structures we know as chromosomes. Two centrioles, structures that act like winches or tractors, appear outside of the nucleus. They have protein spindles that attach to the chromosomes and pull them away from the center line, causing them to migrate to opposite sides of the cell. Before they can do that, the membrane around the nucleus dissolves. Assisted by the spindles, the chromosome pairs line up across from each other along a line of force that appears straight across the very middle (*b'toch*) in the center of the cell. One each of the pair in the doubled chromosomes is then drawn away from its counterpart, each to the opposite end of the cell, while the cell membrane is stretched and elongated. Once that migration takes place, the cell splits down the center, producing a second cell membrane, separating into two new identical cells, divided exactly in two. This is the *rakiya* at work—enabling life.

The above is different from the process known as meiosis. Meiosis is the term applied to the process of cell division that produces cells that have newly recombined DNA information in half the usual number of chromosomes. These are the cells that combine with other cells of like kind to produce a cell with a full complement of DNA—a fertilized egg. They are known as gametes in animals, including humans. The most familiar example of this merger is an egg from a woman and sperm from a man. The process of cell division in meiosis, once the chromosomes have been halved, is the same as mitosis in terms of the stages and the mechanisms. There is a line of division, there are spindles, and there are two resulting haploid (half the number of a regular complement of chromosomes) cells that result. The *rakiya*, the Principle of Division, is again orchestrating it all.

In a human being, this is a new potential life. First comes division and then comes separation. This is true in mitosis and meiosis. The *rakiya* has left its calling card again. This most necessary form of reproduction is clearly the child of the principle of division and separation. The final destination, so to speak, of the division that generates meiosis, however, is for each haploid cell (egg and sperm in us) to find its mate. We will discuss this step in the manifestation of duality in the final verse of *yom sheini*.

Finally, our Sages say that the Splitting of the Sea after the exodus of the Jewish people from Egypt was set in place at Creation. The workings of the *rakiya* are the root of the division and separation of **this** water from water when the sea split. Thus, the *rakiya* enabled the creation of the Jewish nation, extracted from the Egyptian nation. This also mirrors the extraction of the light that came from the darkness of the original singularity in the first moments of Creation.

CHAPTER SIXTEEN

YOM SHEINI: SECOND VERSE, FIRST CONCEIT

ויאמר אלקים יהי רקיע בתוך המים ויהי מבדיל בין מים למים.
ויעש אלקים את הרקיע ויבדל בין המים אשר מתחת לרקיע
ובין המים אשר מעל לרקיע ויהי כן. ויקרא אלקים לרקיע
שמים ויהי ערב ויהי בקר יום שני.

FIRST CONCEIT

ויעש אלקים את הרקיע.
[A]nd God made the rakiya.

This verb, *ya'as* (יעש), is used to reference something that is being fashioned from some previously existing material. This is, as discussed much earlier, not equivalent to nor similar to the verb *bara*, but, rather, almost an antonym. In this case it is fair to ask of our text, "From what is the *rakiya* being fashioned in this phrase?" The answer is that it is being fashioned from itself. That is, it is indicative of a further step toward the permanent status of the physical configuration of the universe. As such, what was previously much closer to being an abstraction, the template of the Principle of Division for the generation of the universe, the *rakiya* is now beginning to evidence itself physically and is on the verge of acquiring permanence. As we are still in the realm of God's creating and fashioning the universe, it seems brilliantly fitting that it is *Elokim* Who is fashioning the *rakiya*. There could be nothing better to exemplify the acts of *Elokim* as the Distinguisher of Distinctions than to generate and then fashion the Principle of Division into a permanent fixture of a physical world.

The other main feature of this phrase is *et ha'rakiya* (את הרקיע). As discussed at length in chapter 4, and here quoting Rabbeinu Bachya ben Asher again, "Whenever the word *et* (את) appears, it adds something to the meaning of the plain text." It is surely the case that this phrase could have been constructed without the *et* and still conveyed the exact same meaning on a simple level. However, as we are within the first two *yamim*, the simple level won't suffice for our analysis. Fortunately, God has led us to dig deeper for what we can be learning about Creation by using this simple little two letter word to reference us to what hides behind the plain text of this phrase.

Conclusively, by examining the world and its wild diversity, we nevertheless find recurring, conforming, congruent patterns throughout the manifestations of physical existence. As mentioned earlier, the Fibonacci sequence recurs again and again throughout the natural world, manifesting as spirals in natural patterns. Bilateral symmetry occurs in much of the animal kingdom, and spectacular embryological similarities are found across extremely diverse species. *Et* is the message prompting us to probe for and find the workings of the *rakiya* everywhere in our world.

Somewhat paraphrased, the Rambam says in *The Guide for the Perplexed*,[37]

> [T]hose who understand the blending of the natural and the Divine are like royal subjects being within the throne room of their exalted king, while those seeking an understanding of the Bible but lacking an understanding of the natural sciences are subjects groping in vain for the outermost gate of the king's palace.

---

37   Moses Maimonides, *The Guide for the Perplexed* (New York: Dover, 1956), part III, ch. 51; also in *Hilchot Yesodei HaTorah* (New York: Moznaim, 1989), 4:10.

Bearing in mind what the Rambam says, perhaps we can take note of the words of Rabbeinu Bachya Ibn Pekudah which we find in his masterwork, *Duties of the Heart (Mind)*, as interpolated by Rabbi Avigdor Miller. In the first gate (*shaar*), *Shaar HaBechinah* he says, "But what is *bechinah*? Essentially, *bechinah* means pondering the signs of Hashem's wisdom that are apparent in nature and analyzing them to the best of the intellectual ability of the *mavchin* (person doing the *bechinah*)." Further, Rabbeinu Bachya asks, "Do we have an obligation to study nature or not? We say that we are duty-bound to study created things to find proof in them of the Creator's wisdom." Lastly, Rabbeinu Bachya goes on to say, "[B]ecause common sense testifies that the superiority of a person over an animal is because of his greater insight and understanding and his ability to grasp the secrets of wisdom that fill the universe."

The phrase we are discussing just now, found within the next to last verse of the eight verses in the first two *yamim*, contains two words that change everything: *ya'as* (יעש) and *et* (את). With the making (*ya'as*) of the *rakiya*, we are being moved into a state of permanence. With the word *et* referencing the *rakiya*, we are being asked to look behind the multiplicity of the manifestations of Creation. Behind the curtain of multiplicity, we find the *rakiya* at work everywhere that it matters, for the sake of the appearance of life itself. This almost transcends time, as the implementation of the making of the *rakiya* began with the generation of matter in favor of anti-matter all the way through to the creation of the membranes that enclose the cells that give life in our world.

CHAPTER SEVENTEEN

YOM SHEINI: SECOND VERSE, SECOND CONCEIT

ויאמר אלקים יהי רקיע בתוך המים ויהי מבדיל בין מים למים.
ויעש אלקים את הרקיע ויבדל בין המים אשר מתחת לרקיע
ובין המים אשר מעל לרקיע ויהי כן. ויקרא אלקים לרקיע
שמים ויהי ערב ויהי בקר יום שני.

SECOND CONCEIT

ויבדל בין...

[A]nd separated between...

Scan through the verses from *yom echad* and *yom sheini* that we have
reviewed so far while also bearing in mind the verses from *yom echad*
in which the name *Elokim* appears. Finally, recognize the eighth verse
and let all of the noted highlights illustrated here, as well as those not
explicitly shown here, sink in for a moment.

> Third Verse:
>
> **וירא אלקים את האור כי טוב ויבדל אלקים**
> **בין האור ובין החשך..**
>
> Fifth Verse:
>
> **ויאמר אלקים יהי רקיע בתוך המים והי מבדיל**
> **בין מים למים.**

Sixth Verse:

ויעש אלקים את הרקיע ויבדל בין המים אשר מתחת
לרקיע ובין המים אשר מעל לרקיע ויהי כן.

Eighth Verse:

ויקרא אלקים לרקיע שמים ויהי ערב ויהי בקר יום שני.

Every one of the terms from the Hebrew text that is bolded has to do with the field of play of duality. Of the ninety-one words in the first two *yamim*, twenty-seven are these kinds of words, not all of which are shown above. That is just shy of thirty percent of all of the words in the first two *yamim* that are words devoted to conveying ideas or abstractions of distinctions, divisions, separations, or clear references to duality! Each one either establishes the distinguishing out of distinctions (*Elokim*), dividing (e.g., *rakiya*), separating (*yavdil* or *bein*), or is alluding to or is a direct reference to a kind of a statement about the reality of, or the nature of, duality (e.g., *shamayim*). The very essence of the entire second *yom* is actually summed up in these two words alone: *va'yavdil bein* (ויבדל בין). This small phrase is the statement that is congruent with all of the bolded words or the essence of their natures.

Our reality, through the perceptions permitted by the normal operations of a fully functioning human nervous system is that of division, separation, and the experience of I/Thou. This universe of ours was made for two and we are the beneficiaries. With these two simple words (*va'yavdil bein*), the charge of the *rakiya* is set, established, and stands on the cusp of permanence, for our sake. If there was no "us," there would be no point to any of it at all. This rests in part on an idea in cosmological physics known as the anthropic principle in which it is posited that the universe had to produce reflective consciousness in order that it itself could be recognized. In concert with this discussion, in the Ramban, on page 32, the translator cites a reference to Rabbi Avraham Ibn Ezra, when he says, "And the meaning of 'and (God) separated' is through assigning of names." The hanging of linguistic labels separates whatever is named from everything else, cementing the nature of this/not-this into Creation. Further, it is well to realize that according to

Heisenberg's uncertainty principle, that which is under observation is influenced by the observer. One could take this to what may seem to be an absurd extreme, to question and then ask, "If there were no human observers with the power of intelligent speech bound up with the naming of distinctions, would there be a universe at all?"

CHAPTER EIGHTEEN

YOM SHEINI: SECOND VERSE, THIRD CONCEIT

ויאמר אלקים יהי רקיע בתוך המים ויהי מבדיל בין מים למים.
ויעשׂ אלקים את הרקיע ויבדל בין המים אשר מתחת לרקיע
ובין המים אשר מעל לרקיע ויהי כן. ויקרא אלקים לרקיע
שמים ויהי ערב ויהי בקר ויהי יום שׁני.

THIRD CONCEIT

המים אשר מתחת לרקיע ובין המים אשר מעל לרקיע.
[T]he water(s) beneath the rakiya and between the water(s)
above the rakiya.

In chapter 2, I noted that when the Maharal of Prague introduced the notion that the abstraction of six was determining the six directions of three-dimensional space, he specifically did not designate their orientations. That is, he did not specify the dichotomies of left/right, front/back and up/down. Said another way, he was maintaining that no orientation of position of a fixed kind existed at that stage of things. This phrase within this verse is declaring that **now** is the point at which positions become fixed, as directions take on the role for orientation, and are now made to exist on a permanent basis. The six designations of up and down, front and back, and left and right sides come into existence and become fixed permanently into the fabric of the universe. For each of us, using our innate sense of orientation in space, it's obvious that the six directions of three-dimensional space would be designated with those three paired spatial labels. This is because, perceptually, each of us has an experience of being in the midst of everything around. So, of course there would be left/right, front/back and up/down.

What our attention is drawn to here is comprised of three features: (1) water; (2) the directions of up and down; and (3) the Principle of Division itself. The narrative is maneuvering this new reality into a condition of solidity. What we are focusing on is the separation of water from water, in what to us is a vertical axis, through the "action" of the *rakiya*. Here, as with the discussion of the *rakiya* itself, we are seeking physical evidence for the operations of **a** *rakiya*, separating water from water, which is being displayed via a vertical orientation. As before, in the spirit of *bechinah*, we look for physical evidence, available for scrutiny through our senses so that we can identify the archetypal template hiding behind the manifestation. This is, by all accounts, the means by which the Patriarch Abraham realized that there was one God.

The notion that there is a correlation between the non-physical (some would call it the metaphysical) world and the physical world and vice versa is an ancient one. It has been given many names, amongst them "microcosm/macrocosm," "as above/so below," etc. As stated in my prefatory material, if God's fingerprints are all over Creation, we should be able to find this pattern of water divided and separated from water in a vertical orientation in more than one instance. I offer two striking examples of this phenomenon, each of which is related to the other.

We can now come back to the earth's layers of water which were discussed in chapter 15, albeit from a different perspective. We are going to add a couple of features to our previous discussion as we examine the nature of the rhythm of the earth's water cycle and the *rakiya*'s role in it. Water vapor from the surface of the earth rises, cools, and forms clouds. Rain, snow, or hail fall onto the land, into the seas, or become added to the ice on earth once the clouds become supersaturated and shed their moisture. Once vaporized from the solid or liquid state on the earth's surface into the gaseous state, the water vapor rises to accumulate and form new clouds. The hallmark of the water cycle is motion from below to above and above to below.

Earlier, as I introduced the understanding of the *rakiya* as the Principle of Division, we were concentrating on the power of dividing, in and of itself. Here we want to focus on what is being divided from what, in a vertical axis: i.e., water above separated from water below. The image we want to focus on is, as the Torah narrative says, "[A]nd separated between the waters which were beneath the *rakiya* and the waters which were above the *rakiya*." Two features make this stand out. First, there is water above and water below. Second, they have a relationship with each other born of a former unity before they were divided. In terms of the relationship of above and below, we are observing phase transitions of water: solid or liquid to gas and back. This is the nature of the power of the boundary between the surface water or ice and the water in the atmosphere: the *rakiya*.

Additionally, a stunning new discovery about the earth's water has just recently been announced. At a depth of 250 to 400 miles below the surface of the earth, water has been found in great abundance. So much so, that were the findings to be validated as being universal throughout the world, over and above the region in North America where the discovery was made, there would be up to three times the amount of water trapped in the rocky structure at that depth than in all of the surface water in the seas, oceans, rivers, and lakes. The chemical structure of the water found at that depth is dictated by the extremes of temperature (hot) and pressure (enormous). That is, the water molecules are in the form of what are called hydroxyl radicals (the OH part of H_2O [H-O-H]), trapped by and chemically bound to the minerals of the mantle rocks in which they were found. Scientists had long speculated that water is trapped in a rocky layer of the earth's mantle located between the lower mantle and upper mantle. Northwestern geophysicist Steve Jacobsen and University of New Mexico seismologist Brandon Schmandt are the first to provide direct evidence that there may be water in this area of the mantle, known as the "transition zone," on a regional scale.

The use of the term transition zone is reminiscent of the nature of phase transitions. Notice the use of the words *between, upper mantle* and *lower mantle, water,* and *layer*. We are certainly dealing with water that is dramatically below the water above. That is, this water is far below all of the other water on earth, that being found distributed in the seas and oceans, etc., combined with the water in the atmosphere. The depth of the liquid water in oceans and seas, etc., when combined with the height of the water vapor in the atmosphere is approximately fifteen miles at most. It is divided and separated from this trapped, enclosed water that has recently been discovered by hundreds of miles. The upper water is separated from the lower water here as well. In Psalm 33, in our morning prayers on the Sabbath, we find, "He places the deep waters in vaults." These deep waters just discussed being hundreds of miles below the surface of the earth are, in fact, locked into the rock formations, bound chemically to the minerals in the rocks. The words used in science and in Scripture are virtually identical.

From the perspective of Chinese medicine, the relationship between the lungs and kidneys in regard to their governance over water in the human body is consistent with the relationship we find between the water on the surface of the earth and the water in the troposphere. The lungs are known as the "upper source of water." The kidneys are known as the "lower source of water." The understanding of the lungs is that in addition to governing respiration, the lungs condense and direct fluids from higher in the body (above the diaphragm) down to the kidneys and bladder for excretion or reabsorption. Determining the *yin* and *yang* basis of these phenomena using the positions of above and below along the vertical axis, we see that the fluids in the upper portion of the body are more *yang*. They are also likened to being a mist. Therefore, they more closely resemble the water vapor in the atmosphere, which is also more *yang* on the basis of position and density.

In contrast, the more-dense fluid state of the waters in the oceans and seas, etc., correlates with the water below the diaphragm in the human body. By virtue of being below in their position along the vertical axis, along with their being of greater density, they are to be seen and understood as being more *yin*. The kidneys vaporize the denser water from below the diaphragm and send it upward to the lungs in order that they may moisten the more superficial layers of the body between the skin and the muscles. Using the Chinese medical view, there is complete congruence in comparing the earth's water cycle with the human water cycle.

The arbiter of the phase transition in this rhythm of water movement in the body is the diaphragm, the human version of the *rakiya* in relation to the water cycle of the earth. The global water cycle and the human water cycle are both governed by a *rakiya*. In the global scenario, the thickness is the distance between the stuck-together teacups, and far less tangible. In the human being, the diaphragm is far thicker than that, yet still very flattened out (not withstanding the dome-shaped configuration of its shape) and thin, relatively speaking. The global and human water cycles are parallel manifestations of the water beneath the *rakiya* and the water above the *rakiya*. As above, so it is below. Congruence is satisfied and macrocosm and microcosm are reflective of each other.

CHAPTER NINETEEN

YOM SHEINI: SECOND VERSE, FOURTH CONCEIT

ויאמר אלקים יהי רקיע בתוך המים ויהי מבדיל בין מים למים. ויעש אלקים את הרקיע ויבדל בין המים אשר מתחת לרקיע ובין המים אשר מעל לרקיע ויהי כן. ויקרא אלקים לרקיע שמים ויהי ערב ויהי בקר יום שני.

FOURTH CONCEIT

ויהי כן.

[A]nd it was so.

These two simple words (in the Hebrew) of so few letters are the cement that holds all of Creation together as a perpetually ongoing enterprise. Through them, permanence is declared and implemented, simply through the power of the narrative itself. This speaks volumes, yet its simplicity mostly overwhelms the need to say more. These six letters cause the physical world's parameters to crystallize, just as God created six with the *tzimtzum* at the very beginning of the Torah. This is the necessary and sufficient condition for the power of division and separation to undergo one last change while becoming, in the process of its making, the *rakiya*. This is the subject of the next verse.

CHAPTER TWENTY

YOM SHEINI: THIRD VERSE, FIRST CONCEIT

ויאמר אלקים יהי רקיע בתוך המים ויהי מבדיל בין מים למים. ויעש אלקים את הרקיע ויבדל בין המים אשר מתחת לרקיע ובין המים אשר מעל לרקיע ויהי כן. ויקרא אלקים לרקיע שמים ויהי ערב ויהי בקר יום שני.

FIRST CONCEIT

ויקרא אלקים.

God called or God called to or God named.

We've encountered this exact same pair of words in chapter 11 in our discussion of the first *yom*. At that time, I surmised that this phrase is subject to three different possible interpretations. There are apparently no commentators who cite a different approach than what is used to understand this in the first *yom*. Either it is "God called" or it is "God called to" or "God named." On the first *yom*, God gave the light and the darkness names. Once Adam himself had been created, he gave names to the various objects of the world (discrete created entities of all sorts, particularly the animals). Since the conditions here also precede Adam coming into being, it is God Who is giving a new name to the *rakiya*.

This newly permanent label produces a remade but different identity for the *rakiya*. Additionally, it reconfigures the nature of the *rakiya* as a function of the relationship between it and *shamayim*. The act of using this linguistic descriptor, in the act of calling, links not only the words that are used, but also their natures. What is the meaning of this new condition as they are now both changed in the very act of their being associated as one identity? To answer this, we need to recall that the *rakiya* has now been made (*ya'as*) instead of solely been spoken into existence. This is completely consistent with the "stepping down" of the acts of Creation into more and more physical forms. Clearly, the act of naming establishes this new reality and makes something new from the previously existing *rakiya*. By virtue of this change, it also remakes *shamayim*.

CHAPTER TWENTY-ONE

YOM SHEINI: THIRD VERSE, SECOND CONCEIT

ויאמר אלקים יהי רקיע בתוך המים ויהי מבדיל בין מים למים.
ויעשׁ אלקים את הרקיע ויבדל בין המים אשׁר מתחת לרקיע
ובין המים אשׁר מעל לרקיע ויהי כן. ויקרא אלקים לרקיע
שׁמים ויהי ערב ויהי בקר יום שׁני.

SECOND CONCEIT

לרקיע שׁמים.

[Called] the rakiya "shamayim."

If we recall the nature of *shamayim* from the very beginning of the first *yom*, *Elokim* kneaded together fire (*aish*, אשׁ) and water (*mayim*, מים) to create *shamayim*. Those primeval, archetypal abstractions, fire and water, pre-existed *shamayim*. Under the conditions described in the first *yom*, this was the ultimate merger of opposites. This was the conjoining of complementary but opposite, yet interdependent, abstract ideational emblems. *Aish* and *mayim* detail the dual inner nature of *shamayim*, and connect us again with the deepest nature of duality itself through this improbable kneading together of the most fundamentally opposite forces. Contrariwise, the nature of the *rakiya* is to divide and separate. In the *Zohar* it says, "So long as the upper and lower waters were commingled, there was no production in the world; this could only be when they were separated and made distinct. They then produced..."[38] With the advent of division and separation (the *rakiya*), the merging of the distinct opposites (*aish* + *mayim* = *shamayim*) can bring about the synergy arising from division, the necessary condition for offspring (manifestation) to come into being.

Shamayim and *rakiya* are essentially antonyms, yet they've now been identified by God as being the same as each other. This is the essence of the paradox that closes out the second *yom*: division and unity, separated and merged, one and two. Among the human urges that we all live with is the drive for the identity of the separate "I," coexisting simultaneously with the yearning to reunite and merge with our Creator and His unity. With the making of the *rakiya* and then identifying it as being *shamayim*, characteristics of the paradox of being human are captured eloquently and simply. From Chinese medicine, we have within us a primeval fire and primeval water. In the function of the economy of the *qi*, they are found at a profoundly fundamental level, being harbored together in the depth of us. They are synergistically merged and they are separated, simultaneously. This paradox is the essence of our existence as physical human beings.

The nature of the human mind shows the manifestation of the dichotomy of the *rakiya* and *shamayim*. Division and separation are the prime functions of our left brain hemisphere. The right hemisphere is responsible for unifying the elements of sensory existence into one of seamlessly connected consciousness with all of existence. I believe recognizing this duality is what is most critical to conclude from our lengthy exposition of the first two *yamim*: we are two selves in two worlds. We are a separate "I" in a world of distinctions and separation. We are a merged self, connected to the entire universe. Ultimately, these two selves are the vehicle God chose for us to play out the human endeavour sparked by the imperative of having free will. Choice is the raison d'être for our existence and choice is always made of this and not-this. The whole universe is made for two.

---

38   Sperling, *The Zohar*, p. 75.

CHAPTER TWENTY-TWO

YOM SHEINI: THIRD VERSE, THIRD CONCEIT

ויאמר אלקים יהי רקיע בתוך המים ויהי מבדיל בין מים למים.
ויעש אלקים את הרקיע ויבדל בין המים אשר מתחת לרקיע
ובין המים אשר מעל לרקיע ויהי כן. ויקרא אלקים לרקיע
שמים ויהי ערב ויהי בקר יום שני.

THIRD CONCEIT

ויהי ערב ויהי בקר יום שני.

And it was erev and it was boker a second yom.

For the sake of review to refresh our perspective, the following are excerpts from Rabbi Samson Raphael Hirsch's Torah commentary and Clark's *Etymological Dictionary of Biblical Hebrew*, based on the writings of Hirsch.

From the etymology as compiled by Matityahu Clark:

Erev (ערב)—*Mix substances with no change in character; (1) mixing without being integrated; (2) darkening; (5) evening; mixed shades of light; (6) twilight*

Boker (בקר)—*Distinguishing difference; (1) examining; (4) morning; time of distinguishing*

From Rabbi Hirsch's Torah commentary, cited above:

> *Erev (*ערב*), where the two conditions begin to mix, and boker,*
> *(*בקר*) related to* בבר, בגר, פקר*, to be free, independent, where*
> *things separate from each other and appear in their own outline*
> *and it is already possible* לבקר*, to distinguish one from the other.*

Once again, as with the first *yom*, we must get past the simple meaning (*p'shat*), which is such a lure, to prevent us from believing that the narrative is describing the sun rising and setting in this verse. Until the fourth *yom*, there are no stars, nor are there any planetary bodies which can have mornings and evenings. Obviously, since *erev* and *boker* are opposites, they conform to the idea that the whole universe is a construct that is consistent with the frame of duality: *yin* and *yang*. A condition of mixing (and being undistinguished) is *erev*, which is relatively *yin*, and a condition of distinguishing differences is *boker*, which is relatively *yang*.

The second *yom* is necessary for *erev* and *boker* to become and remain distinct as separate elements of Creation. Hence, we have the words (*vayehi chein,* ויהי כן). This is the work of the *rakiya*. Yet, now that the *rakiya* has become identified as *shamayim*, we see a flawless reflection of the congruence of *erev* with *shamayim* and *boker* with the *rakiya*. *Erev* and *shamayim* both impart the notion of a mixture and the confounding of details, and *boker* and *rakiya* reveal the distinguishing of distinctions. The language and context match perfectly. With this final phrase in the second *yom*, duality has now become cemented into place as a permanent shaper of the forces of our reality. However, with the identity one to the other of the *rakiya* and *shamayim*, paradox also reigns: How can merging (the kneading together of fire and water) be equated with dividing and separating?

By the conclusion of the second *yom*, duality is sustained and perpetuated as the essence of all emerging phenomena of existence. All the while this is so, however, the unity of God is behind the veil that separates duality, which has the apparency of being the "true" view of Creation for us, from the Creator. *Yom sheini*, this second ascendance (using Hirsch's interpretation of the word *yom*), produces the further concretization of Creation. Now the progression of manifestation aimed toward the advent of a physical world has taken on the required characteristics for the initiation of a complete state change. The change that takes place with the closure of the second *yom* is the consummation of the trajectory from the utterly abstract to the threshold of materialization. The *Midrash Rabbah* describes it linguistically in the following way:

> [T]he word *sheini*, שֵׁנִי, second, being [is] cognate with *shinui*, שִׁינוּי, change.[39]

With the use of *vayehi chein* (ויהי כן) in this *yom*, the entire enterprise of Creation has shifted and changed to establish the conditions necessary for the appearance of actual physical-ness. Henceforward, the progression up the ladder of manifestation is taking place *yom* by *yom*. Once through the remaining *yamim*, all is set in place in order for Man and Woman to assume their roles.

The entire enterprise of Creation has given us the pairs shown below in the progression to its culmination. The break in the array takes place once God **makes** (*ya'as*, יעש) the *rakiya*, at which point everything takes on the new character, with the permanence of division and separation in place. The materialization of the entire world then proceeds to its ultimate goal. The critical pairs of our narrative look like this:

Creator	created
one	two
hyule of heaven	*hyule* of earth
aish	*mayim*
heaven	earth
tohu	*bohu*
ohr	*choshech*
yom	*laylah*

---

39   Blinder, *Midrash Rabbah*, vol. I, ch. 4, p. 7[1], "Insights."

rakiya	*shamayim*
boker	*erev*
Man	Woman

After the seventh *yom*, Man and Woman, for whom the entirety of Creation was apparently generated, come to take their place in the cosmos. Together they are one of the myriad pairs of opposites for which the entire universe was made. The establishment of an identity between the *rakiya* and *shamayim* reiterates the paradox of being joined and divided simultaneously. The design apparent in us is reflective of the same paradox. That is, we are physical and spiritual, and those two natures are a yoked pair. Man and Woman are who they are because we are living within the paradox of our existence. We are embedded in and must negotiate the realities of living in "a universe made for two."

EPILOGUE

IT IS SO easy for us to take life for granted. It is surpassingly simple to just live and never reflect on life. However, in applying consciousness to our daily lives and recognizing the roots of our own existence, we have the potential to have a relationship with the world that yields spectacular results. The manner in which the entire universe was constructed has not a single accident of happenstance in it. It is pure design. It took a lot of "work" on God's part, so to speak, to get it to the point that conscious, reflective, sentient beings could live and thrive in a universe full of extremes and within the parameters of spirit and matter that compete for supremacy. Just the right kind and amount of matter was required to meet the proper parameters of design for certain stars. After building up elements like iron, cobalt, carbon, and magnesium in their cores, derived from fused hydrogen and helium nuclei, those stars needed to explode. This was necessary in order to spew those atoms into the universe so we could have them for use in our planets and our bodies. This dynamic, spanning billions of years, is well beyond pure genius. We have iron in the middle of our red blood cells and rely on cobalt in the middle of vitamin B_{12}. Chlorophyll has magnesium at its center, carbon makes up the sugars needed for metabolism, etc. That's a lot of work.

I only hope that by exploring the first two *yamim* of Creation, from the perspective offered within these pages, a different little glimpse into the sheer brilliance of the Torah and our Creator has been opened. As we've reviewed the evidence for God's fingerprints in Creation, I hope we've shared in the wonder and given pause to reflect on who and how we are, after all. To cite Rabbeinu Bachya Ibn Pekudah again: "Do we have an obligation to study nature or not? We say that we are duty-bound to study created things to find proof in them of the Creator's wisdom." The genesis of Creation through Torah and nature is the story of a universe made for two.

The duality from which God made us and in which our existence persists grants us the ability to distinguish distinctions. Thereby, it gives us the power to choose between opposites at all times. The programming of the left brain, geared as it is for the survival and persistence of the identity called "I," has purpose. Its counterpart, the right brain, also has its purpose. They are meant to have harmonious, synergistic governance over our moment-to-moment existence. We are literally of two minds, and they are yoked to each other inseparably, as Jill Bolte Taylor so eloquently explains while describing her own left hemisphere stroke and her reflections on it. Appendix B is a brief exposition of the two minds we possess.

I also hope that this exploration of the first two *yamim* has given a valuable peek into the power of Chinese medicine and how compatible it is with our deepest spiritual origins. The synergy I've been living with while researching and writing this work is sometimes difficult to articulate—it is so much of a background of my own perspectives on a day-to-day basis for me, as it has been in most respects for forty-five years. Many is the time that the fish truly cannot distinguish the water in which it swims. However, this convergence of Torah exegesis, Chinese medicine theory, geometry, biology, chemistry, quantum mechanics, particle physics, string theory, astrophysics, cosmology, and *Kabbalah* has been captivating, as I have been toiling away in Torah over the last ten years on this project. The parallels between, intersections of, and illuminations cast from one discipline to the others and vice versa, are the catalysts for the synthesis which has grown into what I've written. I trust that it has had merit and proved worthy of the expenditure of your time.

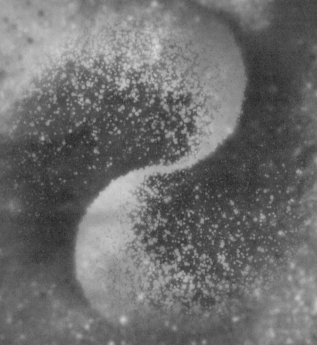

SECTION III

APPENDICES

THE GEOMETRIC CONSTRUCTION OF THE WORLD

THE FIRST WORD of the Torah is *bereishit* (בראשית), which, through a kabbalistic convention discussed at some length in the Ramban's introduction to his Torah commentary, can be transmuted from one six-letter word to become two three-letter words: *bara shēt* (ברא שית). The simple meaning (*p'shat*) of *bereishit* (בראשית) has been the subject of great debate amongst our Sages. However, in permitting the first word to become two words, a clear meaning emerges: "He created six." According to the Maharal, the number six is referring to the six directions of three-dimensional space. This is the resultant of the first "act" of Hashem in creating the world: the generation of the *tzimtzum*. The word *tzimtzum* means restriction or contraction, self-limitation or withdrawal. Kabbalistically, this refers to what God did by withdrawing His all-pervasive supernal light (*Ein Sof*) to the "sides" of a conceptual space in order to create the vacated space into which to create the world. This was the very first aspect of the creation process of bringing the world into existence. The Ari, Rabbi Isaac Luria, in his *Etz Chaim*, says that the *tzimtzum* was a perfect sphere. Now, obviously, no actual perfect physical sphere existed at the beginning of Hashem's creating the world—only the abstraction of it.

In solid geometry, there is an equation that measures the degree to which some solid shape matches a perfect sphere. The resultant of that equation is a measure named sphericity. The *tzimtzum* was such an abstraction, becoming the template for the existence of any perfect sphere in the physical world.

Every perfect sphere has a precise and exact dead center. The Ari goes on to describe that Hashem then drew a thread of His light, the *kav ohr Ein Sof*, into the vacated space. From all renderings of these descriptions, also appearing in other kabbalistic texts, such as the *Bahir*, the thread of light, the *kav*, extended to the exact center of the vacated space.

Let's take stock of where we have gotten to so far. We have the six directions of three-dimensional space, which implies the famous X, Y, and Z axes of geometry. We have a perfect sphere. We have the surface of the sphere and its enclosed space. We have the zero-dimension point at the dead center of the sphere. And, lastly, we have the line that connects the surface of the sphere to the center of the sphere. The center point or any singular point is a zero-dimension entity in mathematics and geometry. The line is a one-dimensional entity. The sphere is a three-dimensional entity. What is apparently missing at this juncture in our discussion is the two-dimensional entity, a plane. However, the plane exists in the form of the surface of the sphere. Recalling that what we think of as physical shapes do not yet exist in physical form at this point in Creation, we have to think big. The age-old question of whether the earth is flat or round was answered many years ago mathematically and then by direct observation when satellites and astronauts first sent back pictures of earth from space. However, experientially, and without benefit of instrumentation, the surface of the earth is flat. For example, we don't adjust our footsteps to account for the curvature of the earth. Only over very long distances does the curvature become a factor for civil and aeronautical engineers. Additionally, as those who invented calculus concluded, the mathematical means by which to assess and operate with a curve is to break it up into an infinite number of flat surfaces.

So now we have all three dimensions and all six directions of three-dimensional space. These elements of geometry are all that is needed to construct a physical world. As an aside, the word geometry and *gematria* have the same root. It is said in *Kabbalah* that, along with the *sefirot*, Hashem used the Hebrew letters to create the world, each one having a numerical value in *gematria*.

Geometrically speaking, when a plane intersects a sphere, the resultant shape is a circle. That is, the location where the two shapes meet has the shape of a perfect circle. Also, as a bit of an aside, the circle has a key role in certain other aspects in the process of Creation, one of the most striking of which is the geometric law that one circle will always have six circles of exactly the same size perfectly touching the circumference and touching their neighbors to either side.

However, let's get back to our circle. If one connects the circle brought out on the surface of the sphere resulting from the intersection of the plane with the sphere to the zero-dimension point at the center of the sphere, one produces a cone. The only exception to this rule is if the plane intersects the sphere while running through the center point of the sphere as well. The importance for this is in the

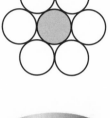

shapes yielded in the process of a cone being intersected by another plane. This is the area of solid geometry known as conic sections. They have been studied since ancient times, and the pursuit of understanding them was undertaken by such luminaries as Ptolemy, Euclid, Johannes Kepler, Isaac Newton, and René Descartes.

What, then, are conic sections, and why are they important? First, the shapes that emerge are circles, ellipses, parabolas, and hyperbolas. The need for circles and the circular principle is obvious: tires, timepieces, rings, ball bearings, Torah scroll spindles, etc. The shapes of the orbit

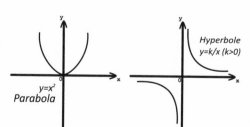

of every planet around its sun, whether in our solar system or another, of every moon around every planet, and the shape of every galaxy, and so forth, are all elliptical. The trajectory of every object propelled from the surface of a celestial body—unless projected straight up, directly overhead—is a parabolic trajectory. This fact is essential for flight, battle, and sport. A hyperbola is, perhaps, a bit more difficult to perceive, since we (mostly) no longer tell time with sundials. The shape traced by the shadow on a sundial is a hyperbola. Navigation at sea in modern times is possible due to the properties of the hyperbola, and it is essential in finding your lost cellphone.

The conclusion, then, is that Hashem created the *tzimtzum* in order to produce certain inherent properties in the world. The properties of it and the *kav ohr Ein Sof* and what results from their interactive relationship are precursor templates. They exist in order to create our physical world as it is. This is revealed through the relationship between the ideational abstractions that God brought into existence in order to create the world with the embodiment of those abstractions established in the structures of the physical world itself.

ABRACADABRA:
I CREATE AS I SPEAK
אברא כ'אדברה

THIS APPENDIX IS included to provide a portion of what I have learned since my dear friend Chaim Schecter asked me the question, "So what?" His question was prompted by my excitedly sharing what I had learned as my writing proceeded through the verses of the first two *yamim*. His point was well taken, as in, What was the use and practicality of what I was telling him? The result is what I am sharing with you here as a scratch-the-surface version of what is to be found in my forthcoming book, *Abracadabra: I Create as I Speak*. It is also a portion of the content in the experiential workshop I have designed called "Trust, Forgiveness and the Path to Peace™," which has provided profound breakthroughs in peacefulness for many of the participants of the workshop.

Just as God spoke the world into existence, we, too, have the power to speak a world into existence, as we are *b'tzelem Elokim*, made in the image of God. Our Sages have alternatively described *b'tzelem Elokim* as signifying that we are speaking beings. However, obviously, our speaking can't build quarks and electrons, nor stars, cows, or whales. Here we are taking speaking to mean all of human ideation, composed of distinctions of language to which meaning has been assigned. Ideation, the act of thinking thoughts, comes in the form of mundane, triggered, reactive thoughts as well as the creative ideas of higher human cognition. Subsequently, any of those thoughts may be verbalized and made audible to others.

What, then, is the difference in the two different versions of human cognition, and how do those thoughts enter into our mouths to be verbalized?

We have two brains, actually two brain hemispheres: left and right. Although their morphology is essentially identical, their modes of function and the regions of pre-assigned responsibilities are clearly different from side to side. The left brain acts like a serial processor in a computer. It deals with the input our nervous systems receive in a linear fashion, whereby it then parses, discriminates, assigns labels, and generates details that are filed away about each of the moments in our lives. The right brain acts like a parallel processor and simultaneously, synergistically integrates all of the sensory energy input that streams into us. It does not assign linguistic labels like the left brain does and does not designate distinctions. Nor does it attach a coherent timeline in the form of a narrative to events and other input, as everything is happening in real time in an all-at-once kind of fashion.

As the right brain has this in-the-moment kind of integrating role in how we interact with our world, we don't usually have access to the "language" of its processing. When we do have this access, the experience is often that which the mystics allude to in an "I'm connected to everything with no sense of self and other" kind of way.

The left brain's function is to categorize and record the present (which, of course instantly becomes the past). It does this to make sure we can negotiate the process of living for the sake of survival of the self (our unique, individual identity) or anything the self considers itself to be (driven by self-talk, whether consciously recognized or not). In addition, it does this so that we can deal with anything new that resembles what we have recorded about the past, in part for survival and in part for maximizing our capabilities. These recorded distinctions are outside of our control, and we can't design or alter what is stored from the past nor can we change that with which any given item of storage is associated. The function of the left brain is constantly on auto-pilot and can't ever be turned off by our will. It is tantamount to being a machine that comes into existence as we are born (perhaps earlier, but we won't go there with this discussion): a pure mechanism of recordation in the language of distinctions about memories, images, thoughts, nostrums, beliefs, interpretations of body sensations, and so on. Its distinctions are drawn on the basis of negation and are formulated in the language in which we are born and raised, in which we are spoken to, and which is with us as we begin the maturation process. We discussed this dynamic at length on page 12 in chapter 2 in the example of the two faces/vase paradox.

Contrast, spoken about at length in chapter 3, particularly on pages 25–40, rests on the essential distinction of this/not-this. Thus, as was also said earlier, contrast—hence the capacity to draw distinctions—relies on negation: something is only recognizable as a function of not-the-something. Some years ago, there was a TV show called *Dinosaurs*, which was about a suburban family of dinosaurs with a mother, father, and three children. The father went to work and the mother stayed at home, and their children consisted of a teenage boy and girl and a baby who was old enough to speak in simplest terms. While riding on his father's shoulders, like we would carry our own children of such an age, the baby would hit his father on the top of the head with a frying pan, vocally proclaiming, "Not the Momma, not the Momma!" Negation is the tool of the left brain as it exercises its capacity to draw distinctions and assign linguistic labels to whatever has been distinctly discerned. If there is no negation, there are no distinctions; no language, no labels. It is negation itself that permits us to have language and to speak with intelligible sounds to another person. Tone and intent are another matter altogether. We will have more on this in the next pages.

The roots of negation are born out of the *challal*. We discussed this at great length in chapter 2, particularly on pages 10–11. We are, therefore, following in God's footsteps, so to speak, insofar as we are cognizing the world of our experience from within the frame of not-this. This comparison is valid on the basis of God having created Creation within what we could term the negation of Himself, which we refer to as the *challal*. God created an entire universe within Himself, by withdrawing His light, creating the vacated space, and leaving behind the created darkness which conforms only to the order He placed in it. It itself was endowed with no creative power of its own.

Our left-brain function is like the *challal*. It is dark, since it can't create but can only react according to the rules embedded in the construction of its neurons, combined with the laid-in record of its history-taking narrative about our lives. Thus, when things spring to mind that are not pondered creative thoughts, they are representatives of the past, coming to determine the meaning of the present and future in service to producing a continuity of identity through our individual narrative. The descriptors in that narrative were put in place by virtue of the power of contrast (negation). However, they are records of past effects whose effecting conditions are no longer in existence. Universally, when they show up, they are then virtually always unexamined as to their worth, applicability, or propriety to serve as a director by which to act or speak in the present. For example, many is the time those messages were put in place when we were children, at a time when we were defenseless against untruths and misapprehensions. It is axiomatic that "truths" initiated for the sake of survival in childhood always turn on their owners in adulthood.

Without exception, we are all subject to the spontaneous, commonly unwelcome, unbidden, negative judging comments from the left brain's narrative about just about anything. For the most part, the chatter is the determiner of the very next triggered series of thoughts, body sensations, emotions, feelings, old self-talk messages, and opinions and judgments about oneself and everything and everybody else. It is a mechanism of reaction to stimuli from an internal or external origin. The result is the same: it reacts and we are the field of play in which the consequences occur. For some, this set of reactions, and reactions to reactions, is like a certain kind of slavery. This is most easily characterized as negative judgments or negative, critical commentary. The apparency is that we are having a conversation (silently in our minds) with ourselves, but we're not really, because one side of the conversation is the machinery of the left brain reacting to whatever comes along. Given this scenario, the description of which is validated by brain research and rigorous experimental evidence, what is the road to freedom from this experience of being entrapped in one's own mind?

There are four potential strategies for dealing with the unwelcome mental chatter. They are as follows: (1) avoidance, e.g., drugs, alcohol, or other preoccupations; (2) agreement; (3) disagreement; and (4) listening without interacting. Avoidance never works because the unwelcome voice never sleeps nor does it need to eat. It will just be there waiting when the avoidance sidetrack concludes. Coming back from the avoidance to face the day, means that the narrative also comes back. To agree with it is to give in to the negation of oneself or something or someone else as the "truth." This doesn't work either. Disagreeing gives credence to the content of the narrative, and the more we argue with it the more it argues with us. This is a recipe for exhaustion. Letting the narrative be, without judging it or agreeing with it or disagreeing with it and without attempting to avoid or cover it over with some other focus of attention, means that it will have no hold over one's mind. This is the only strategy that has power and creativity in it. The response to adopt to the urgings of the reactive mind might be to say (think) to it, "Thank you for sharing. I'm busy right now. Can you come back tomorrow around noon and we'll have lunch together?"

First of all, it's going to come back anyway, because it's preprogrammed to be insistent and persistent. By choosing to engage with it by letting it be, it gives this part of our mind respect, as this manner acknowledges its existence. However, it gives us the power inherent in being the chooser of the type of engagement. This gives us freedom from the confounding companion. When we relate to the triggered reactivity with letting it be, this is the key to the freedom that is possible. It will still chatter away, but we will have disidentified ourselves from it. The language it uses will, to the degree we give it life, govern our experience of reality. The words we speak, even to ourselves in the silence of our own minds, generate the version of reality inside of which we live. This is all the more true for the words we speak to others. Not everything that springs to mind is worthy of being given audible exposure. I endorse the motto, "Don't believe everything you think."

Literally, what we say creates reality. Whether it's what we tell ourselves or it's what we say to others or about others, reality is generated in the listening of the receiver. God creates the world and we create our world. The world that God created came into existence as a function of the cognitive emblems and abstractions He used, which we have discussed in the body of this work. Of course, we have not covered all of His utterances. The world of human experience, however, comes into existence as a function of the labels of language whose meaning is agreed upon by oneself and with others, and which are contextually endorsed. We do, truly, create as we speak, whether to ourselves or to others. The world of human experience awaits, and it is for us to create. God gave us this awesome power to use freely. The consequences of our speaking are those with which we are unavoidably then destined to live. It is not magical, it just seems like it is sometimes. *Abracadabra*— I create as I speak.

THE TZIMTZUM
צ[י]מצום

THE WORD *TZIMTZUM,* meaning restriction or contraction, self-limitation or withdrawal, and which kabbalistically refers to what God did in order to create the "vacated space" into which to create the world, was the very first aspect of the creation process of bringing the world into existence. The root of the word *tzimtzum* is *tzum* (צום). What is the meaning and purpose of the *tzim* of *tzimtzum*? In the body of Hebrew etymology, there seems to be no root word linked to the syllable *tzim*. This relegates the first half of the word *tzimtzum* to being an echoing or mirroring of *tzum,* or, apparently, to being an alliterative emphasis of *tzum.* However, when we examine the structure of the word itself, we see two letters that are identical in each "half" of the word: *tzaddi* (צ) and *mem* (ם). In the first "half" of the word, moving from right to left in the conventional Hebrew construction, we find no letter between the *tzaddi* and the *mem,* and the letter *vav* (ו) between them in the second "half." With the pronunciation of the first syllable being phonetically spelled *tzim,* the meaning, functionality, and etymology is unchanged if the implied vowelization is actually inserted, accomplished by the inclusion of a *yud* (י). This is a convention, related exclusively to the *yud* and *vav,* which is called *malei vechaser* (מלא וחסר), full or defective (this is not a pejorative term), in Hebrew biblical exegesis, often brought to bear by the Baal Haturim, for example, in his Torah commentary. This is a *remez* (a hint), a means by which to allude to and expose meanings and information less obvious than that found in the simple text of the Torah. This is one of the four levels of understanding the Torah:

p'shat (פשט)	simple
remez (רמז)	allusion
drush (דרש)	allegory
sod (סוד)	esoteric

The letter *mem* (ם) needs addressing at some length here. Into the *luchot*, the tablets of the Ten Commandments, two "closed" letters were carved through and through: *samech* (ס) and *mem* (ם). In both instances, the centers of the letters themselves were suspended miraculously, even though the portions of stone that directly surrounded them were missing. This version of the letter *mem* was what we today think of as a final *mem*, the "open" version having been initiated for use in the midst of or at the beginning of a word at the time of the Prophets, as described in the Talmud.[40] However, adopting the premise that the *tzimtzum* was created just before the beginning of time, we will represent that the *mem* (ם) involved in the creation of the abstraction and the word was what we think of today as a final *mem*. Therefore, the two letters *mem* found in *tzimtzum* are both final *mems*.

What I wish to do now, the above having been established, is to rely on a convention having to do with the nature and meaning of the two Hebrew letters, *vav* (ו) and *yud* (י).

The Tetragrammaton (י-ה-ו-ה) is the full name of God in His infinitude, unassociated with any actions, as are some other of God's names. The Rambam refers to this four-letter name as *Shem* (Name) *HaMeforash*[41] in his work *Moreh Nevuchim*, the *Guide for the Perplexed*.[42] In certain contexts, our Jewish Sages consider the Divine Name as having two halves: *yud-hei* (י-ה) and *vav-hei* (ו-ה). There is a practice to

40   Yisroel Schorr, *The Gemara: Tractate Shabbos* (Brooklyn: Mesorah, 1996), vol. 3, ch. 12, p. 104a, fn. 1–3.

41   Latin: *Nomen proprium* - English: A name that belongs to someone or something.

42   Maimonides, *The Guide for the Perplexed*, p. 179.

think of the two-letter name Y-H (י-ה) as being more associated with matters pertaining to God Himself alone. For example, in the domain of the rectification (*tikkun*) of the world, the two-letter name Y-H (י-ה) has to do with God's role, and the V-H (ו-ה) has more to do with that for which human beings are responsible. Notice that the only difference in the two "halves" of God's ineffable Name are in the letters *yud* (י) and *vav* (ו), the *yud* appearing in the first half and the *vav* appearing in the second half.

What I am proposing here is far more than a coincidence of word construction. The word *tzimtzum* has two halves, identical with each other except for the (inserted) *yud* in the first half and the *vav* in the second half. The Tetragrammaton has two halves, identical with each other except for the *yud* in the first half and the *vav* in the second half. In principle, the two words are identical in structure.

The *gematria* for the letter *yud* is ten and for the letter *vav* is six. The discussion earlier of the first two words (kabbalistically speaking) of the Torah (ברא שית) is that they mean "He created six." Six is referring to the six directions of three-dimensional space, the nature of the vacated space referred to above. It is axiomatic in kabbalistic thought that the essential means by which God created the world was through the advent of the *sefirot* (emanations, indicating the emanation of light from the Almighty), of which there are ten. Therefore, the word *tzimtzum* (צימצום), in what I believe could be its full (מלא) form, is reflective of the ten *sefirot* in heaven and the six directions of three-dimensional space in the (created) world. The match of the dual nature of the physical arrangement of the letters of *tzimtzum* with those of the Tetragrammaton is itself a *remez* of the congruence of God's essence juxtaposed with the conditions He brought into existence for the creation of the world. This is revealed through the relationship between the ideational abstractions that God brought into existence in order to create the world with the embodiment of those abstractions established in the structures of the physical world itself.

BIBLIOGRAPHY

Adee, Sally. "Shock and Awe." *The Week*, 6 Apr. 2012:40–41.

Alter, Michael J. *Why the Torah Begins with the Letter Beit*. Northvale, NJ: Jason Aronson, 1998.

Aviezer, Nathan. *In the Beginning: Biblical Creation and Science*. Hoboken, NJ: Ktav Publishing House, 1990.

Ben Asher, Bachya, trans. Eliyahu Munk. *Midrash Rabbeinu Bachya: Torah Commentary*, vols. 1, 6, 7. Jerusalem: Lambda, 2003.

Blinder, Yaakov, and Ben Tzion Gliksberg, et al. *Sefer Bereishis: The Midrash: Midrash Rabbah, with an Annotated, Interpretive Elucidation and Additional Insights, Bereishis–Noach*, vol. 1, chaps. 1–4. Brooklyn, NY: Mesorah Publications, 2014.

Brown, Dan. *The Lost Symbol: A Novel*. New York: Doubleday, 2009.

Clark, Matityahu, and Samson Raphael Hirsch. *Etymological Dictionary of Biblical Hebrew: Based on the Commentaries of Rabbi Samson Raphael Hirsch*. Jerusalem: Feldheim Publishers, 1999.

Dan, Joseph, and Ronald C. Kiener. *The Early Kabbalah*. New York: Paulist, 1986.

Eisemann, Moshe M. and Tiby Segal. *Le-talmidim Ha-me'ayenim = For Rashi's Thoughtful Students: An Attempt to Learn How to Learn Rashi's Immortal Chumash Commentary*. Baltimore, MD: Moshe M. Eisemann, 2010.

Engelson, Morris. "Science Catches Up to Shavuos." *Mishpacha*, June 5, 2011.

Fine, Lawrence. *Safed Spirituality: Rules of Mystical Piety, the Beginning of Wisdom*. New York: Paulist, 1984.

Goldfinger, Andrew. *Thinking about Creation: Eternal Torah and Modern Physics*. New York, NY: Rowman & Littlefield, 1999.

Goldwurm, Hersh, Yisroel Simcha Schorr, Michoel Weiner, and Asher Dicker. *Talmud Bavli: The Schottenstein Edition: The Gemara: The Classic Vilna Edition, with an Annotated, Interpretive Elucidation, as an Aid to Talmud Study. Tractate Sanhedrin*, vol. 3, chap. 11. Brooklyn, NY: Mesorah Publications, 2002.

Greene, Brian. *The Elegant Universe: Superstrings, Hidden Dimensions, and the Quest for the Ultimate Theory*. New York: W.W. Norton, 1999.

Gold, Avie. *Baal Haturim Chumash: The Torah with the Baal Haturim's Classic Commentary Translated, Annotated, and Elucidated*, vol. 1. Brooklyn, NY: Mesorah Publications, 1999.

Hawking, Stephen. *A Brief History of Time: From the Big Bang to Black Holes*. Toronto: Bantam, 1988.

Hawking, Stephen. *The Universe in a Nutshell*. New York: Bantam, 2001.

Herzka, Eliezer, Zev Meisels, Abba Zvi Naiman, Yisroel Simcha Schorr, and Chaim Malinowitz. *Tractate Yoma: The Gemara: The Classic Vilna Edition, with an Annotated, Interpretive Elucidation. Tractate Yoma*, vol. 2, ch. 5. Brooklyn, NY: Mesorah Publications, 1998.

Hirsch, Samson Raphael. *The Hirsch Chumash*, vol. 1. Jerusalem: Feldheim Publishers, 2002.

Jastrow, Marcus. *A Dictionary of the Targumim, the Talmud Babli and Yerushalmi, and the Midrashic Literature*. New York: Judaica, 1996.

Kahneman, Daniel. *Thinking, Fast and Slow*. New York: Farrar, Straus and Giroux, 2011.

Kamenetsky, Dovid, Yisroel Simcha Schorr, and Chaim Malinowitz, eds. *Tractate Chagigah: The Gemara: The Classic Vilna Edition, with an Annotated, Interpretive Elucidation, Tractate Chagigah*, Brooklyn, NY: Mesorah Publications, 1999.

Kaplan, Aryeh, and Abraham Sutton. *Innerspace: Introduction to Kabbalah, Meditation and Prophecy*. Jerusalem: Moznaim, 1990.

Kaplan, Aryeh. *Jerusalem, the Eye of the Universe*. New York: National Conference of Synagogue Youth/Union of Orthodox Jewish Congregations of America, 1976.

Kaplan, Aryeh. *Sefer Yetzirah: The Book of Creation*. York Beach, ME: S. Weiser, 1993.

Kaplan, Aryeh, and Neḥunya Ben Ha-Kanah. *The Bahir*. York Beach, ME: S. Weiser, 1989.

Kasher, Menahem M. *Encyclopedia of Biblical Interpretation, a Millennial Anthology*, vol. 1. New York: American Biblical Encyclopedia Society, 1953.

Keown, Daniel. *The Spark in the Machine: How the Science of Acupuncture Explains the Mysteries of Western Medicine*. London: Jessica Kingsley, 2014.

Lao-tzu, and John C.H. Wu. *Tao Teh Ching*. New York: St. John's UP, 1961.

Lavon, Yaakov, Avie Gold, and Nosson Scherman. *The Complete ArtScroll Selichos*. Brooklyn, NY: Mesorah Publications, 1992.

Lieh-tzu, and A.C. Graham. *The Book of Lieh-tzu*. London: Murray, 1960.

Livio, Mario. *The Golden Ratio: The Story of Phi, the World's Most Astonishing Number*. New York: Broadway, 2002.

Maimonides, Moses, and Eliyahu Touger. *Hilchot Yesodei HaTorah = The Laws (which Are) the Foundations of the Torah*. New York: Moznaim Publishing, 1989.

Maimonides, Moses, trans. M. Friedländer. *The Guide for the Perplexed*. New York: Dover Publications, 1956.

Malbim, Meir Loeb ben Jehiel Michael, and Zvi Faier. "Book One." *Malbim: Rabbenu Meir Leibush Ben Yechiel Michel: Commentary on the Torah*. Jerusalem: M.P., 1982.

Maor, Eli. *To Infinity and Beyond: A Cultural History of the Infinite*. Princeton, NJ: Princeton UP, 1991.

Matt, Daniel Chanan. *The Zohar: Pritzker Edition*, vol. 1. Stanford (Calif.): Stanford UP, 2004.

Matt, Daniel Chanan. *Zohar, the Book of Enlightenment*. New York: Paulist, 1983.

Munk, Elie, and Yitzchok Kirzner. *The Call of the Torah: An Anthology of Interpretation and Commentary on the Five Books of Moses: Bereishis*. Brooklyn, NY: Mesorah Publications, 1992.

Munk, Michael L. *The Wisdom in the Hebrew Alphabet: The Sacred Letters as a Guide to Jewish Deed and Thought*. Brooklyn, NY: Mesorah Publications, 1983.

Nachmanides, Moses, trans. Charles B. Chavel. *Commentary on the Torah: Genesis, Deuteronomy*. New York: Shilo, 1999.

Nachmanides, Yaakov Blinder, Yosef Kamenetzky, and Yehudah Bulman. *Ramban: The Torah with Ramban's Commentary*, vol. 1. Brooklyn, NY: Mesorah Publications, 2004.

Scherman, Nosson. *The Complete Artscroll Machzor Yom Kippur*. Liturgy and Ritual. Day of Atonement Prayers. Brooklyn: Mesorah, 1986.

Scherman, Nosson. *Tanach the Stone Edition: The Torah, Prophets, Writings: The Twenty-Four Books of the Bible Newly Translated and Annotated = Tana"k*. Brooklyn, NY: Mesorah Publications, 2003.

Scherman, Nosson, *The Artscroll Siddur, Weekday/Sabbath/Festival*. Brooklyn, NY: Mesorah Publications, 1987.

Schneider, Israel, and Zev Meisels. *Tractate Berachos: The Gemara: The Classic Vilna Edition, with an Annotated, Interpretive Elucidation. Tractate Berachos*, vol. 2. Brooklyn, NY: Mesorah Publications, 1997.

Schneider, Michael S. *A Beginner's Guide to Constructing the Universe: The Mathematical Archetypes of Nature, Art, and Science*. New York, NY: HarperCollins, 1994.

Scholem, Gershom. *Zohar, the Book of Splendor: Basic Readings from the Kabbalah*. New York: Schocken, 1977.

Schorr, Yisroel Simcha, and Abba Zvi Naiman, et al. *Talmud Bavli: The Schottenstein Edition: The Gemara: The Classic Vilna Edition, with an*

Annotated, Interpretive Elucidation, as an Aid to Talmud Study. Tractate Shabbos, vol. 3, chap. 12, 104a, footnotes 1–3. Brooklyn, NY: Mesorah Publications, 1996.

Schroeder, Gerald L. *Genesis and the Big Bang: The Discovery of Harmony between Modern Science and the Bible*. New York: Bantam, 1990.

Seife, Charles. *Zero: The Biography of a Dangerous Idea*. New York: Viking, 2000.

Simmons, Shraga. *Discovery*. Jerusalem: Aish HaTorah, 1996.

Sperling, Harry, Maurice Simon, and Paul P. Levertoff. *The Zohar*, vol. 1. London: Soncino, 1931.

Volosov, Paul. *Havdalah: Between Holy and Profane*. Baltimore: Private Publish. 2009.

Weinberg, Steven. *The First Three Minutes: A Modern View of the Origin of the Universe*. New York: Basic, 1977.

Winston, Pinchas. "Perceptions—Parshas Bereishis, 5766." *Perceptions—Parshas Bereishis, 5766*. Torah.org, Oct. 2005.

Winston, Pinchas. "Perceptions—Parshas Bereishis, 5767." *Perceptions—Parshas Bereishis, 5767*. Torah.org, Oct. 2006.

Winston, Pinchas. "Perceptions—Parshas Bereishis, 5770." *Perceptions—Parshas Bereishis, 5770*. Torah.org, Oct. 2009.

Zlotowitz, Meir. *The Artscroll Tanach Series: Bereishis/Genesis*, section I. Brooklyn, NY: Mesorah Publications, 1986.

ABOUT THE AUTHOR

JACK M. DANIEL, M. Ac.(UK), Lic. Ac., Dipl. Ac. (NCCAOM) received his acupuncture degrees from the College of Traditional Acupuncture in the UK. In 1975, he cofounded the Centre for Traditional Acupuncture in Columbia, MD, and has practiced in Columbia since then. In addition, he has taught advanced education programs for thousands of acupuncturists around the world, and as staff acupuncturist treated patients at the Sydney Kimmel Comprehensive Cancer Care Center at Johns Hopkins Hospital in Baltimore, MD. He lives in Baltimore with his wife, children, and grandchildren.

ABOUT
MOSAICA PRESS

MOSAICA PRESS is an independent publisher of Jewish books. Our authors include some of the most profound, interesting, and entertaining thinkers and writers in the Jewish community today. Our books are available around the world. Please visit us at www.mosaicapress.com or contact us at info@mosaicapress.com. We will be glad to hear from you.